WILLIAM JAMES
ON RADICAL EMPIRICISM
AND RELIGION

# WILLIAM JAMES ON RADICAL EMPIRICISM AND RELIGION

Hunter Brown

UNIVERSITY OF TORONTO PRESS
Toronto Buffalo London

© University of Toronto Press 2012
Toronto   Buffalo   London
www.utppublishing.com


ISBN 978-0-8020-4734-2 (cloth)
ISBN 978-1-4426-1490-1 (paper)

Toronto Studies in Philosophy
Editors: James R. Brown and Calvin Normore

**Canadian Cataloguing in Publication Data**

Brown, Hunter
William James on radical empiricism and religion

(Toronto studies in philosophy)
Includes bibliographical references and index.
ISBN 978-0-8020-4734-2 (bound).   ISBN 978-1-4426-1490-1 (pbk.)

1. James, William, 1842–1910 – Contributions in philosophy of
religion.   2. Religion – Philosophy.   3. Pragmatism.   I. Title.
II. Series.

B945.J24B76 2000      210′.92      C99-932798-4

University of Toronto Press acknowledges the financial assistance to
its publishing program of the Canada Council for the Arts and the
Ontario Arts Council.

This book has been published with the help of a grant from the
Humanities and Social Sciences Federation of Canada, using funds
provided by the Social Sciences and Humanities Research Council of
Canada.

University of Toronto Press acknowledges the financial support for
its publishing activites of the Government of Canada through the
Book Publishing Industry Development Program (BPIDP).

# Contents

WILLIAM JAMES
ON RADICAL EMPIRICISM
AND RELIGION

# Introduction

'Ever not quite.' The phrase represents more succinctly than most the character of James's philosophical outlook. That outlook is geared above all to carefully observing 'the character with which life concretely comes and the expression which it bears of being, or at least of involving, a muddle and struggle, with an "ever not quite" to all our formulas, and novelty and possibility forever leaking in.'[1] A good philosopher is vigilant above all, when creating theory, about protecting novelty and possibility from generalizations and abstractions. The business of the philosopher is, first and foremost, to remain attuned to the fact, as James said through the words of his friend Benjamin Paul Blood, that 'the universe is wild, – game-flavoured as a hawk's wing. Nature is miracle all; the same returns not save to bring the different.'[2] Even that which is different in only small ways must be given its due place in reflection, for its wider significance may far exceed its importance as an individual. 'The slow round of the engraver's lathe gains but the breadth of a hair, but the difference is distributed back over the whole curve, never an instant true, – ever not quite.'[3]

The ever-not-quite-complete character of inquiry and reflection is an ancient and perennial theme in philosophy. It is a theme, however, which emerges in diverse forms in the works of different thinkers. It is not handled by Kierkegaard, for example, as it is by Russell or Rorty. James too is distinctive in the way he draws out its implications. This is especially the case in connection with a peculiar tension between liberty and restraint which characterizes his work on the formation of belief. The liberty involved here has little in common with the liberal permissiveness often imputed to James's position by those who interpret him subjectivistically and fideistically. Such readings are as deeply erroneous as they are widespread. On the contrary, James was deeply committed to the importance in principle of restraining belief, or to the importance of evidence in the responsible conduct of the life of reason.

In fact, James shared much in common on these matters with evidentialists such as W.K. Clifford, to whom he responds in *The Will to Believe*. Both James and Clifford were aware of the inconclusiveness of philosophy. Both were aware of the temptation to believe and theorize beyond what is warranted evidentially and they both realized that resisting this temptation is no easy task. 'This duty is often a hard one,' Clifford warned, 'and the doubt which comes out of it is a very bitter thing. It leaves us bare and powerless where we thought we were safe and strong.'[4] Clifford therefore counselled the rejection of any behaviour which may 'nourish belief by suppressing doubts and avoiding investigation.'[5]

James's philosophy is entirely in accord with such a prohibition. Careful attention to *all* features of the world and experience, regardless of their potentially subversive effect on belief and theory, is the hallmark of James's Radical Empiricism. Such attention undermined many of his own aspirations after theoretical comprehensiveness and personal belief. When experience pointed unexpectedly in materialist or pluralist, rather than in the metaphysical or monistic directions that he had anticipated, for example – or vice versa – he always followed, both theoretically and personally. If parts of his thought remained incongruent or irreconcilable with one another as a result, he left them that way out of respect for the observations that rendered them so.

James's work has often been attacked by critics for the many loose ends which have resulted from this way of proceeding. These have been interpreted as manifestations of his intellectual shortcomings. Actually, they are more often manifestations of the robust form of his empiricism, and the powerful regulative influence of empiricism on his formation of theory and belief. If James is not always entirely consistent at the level of theoretical systematization, it is frequently because he is highly consistent in attending to all phenomena which might in any way be evidentially relevant to a particular line of inquiry.

James's position parts company with that of evidentialists such as Clifford in the vigour with which he pursues the implications of the fact that the 'ever not quite' of rigorous empirical inquiry cuts two ways, not just one. The 'ever not quite' has direct relevance not just for the legitimacy of belief, but also for the legitimacy of doubt. While inquiry on matters such as theism and free will falls short of providing full support for belief, it also fails to provide full support for disbelief as well. What is one to do in such situations?

It has been a staple of philosophical culture to assume that when inquiry falls short of fully supporting belief, intellectual responsibility favours disbelief, or at least a suspension of judgment. Since such disbelief is not itself directly supported by evidence, by what exactly is it supported? The tenacity with which James pressed this issue, and the detailed epistemological work throughout his corpus which has a direct bearing upon it, are distinguishing marks of his philosophy that will be illustrated and frequently defended throughout this book.

On the one hand then, for James, 'after all that reason can do has been done, there still remains the opacity of the finite facts as merely given, with most of their peculiarities mutually unmeditated and unexplained.'[6] On the other hand, however, the individual human being is forced by its inherent historicity, as the existentialists have often argued, to plunge into opacity and make provisional sense of it. There will always be an 'ever not quite' at the heart of this situation. For James, the full significance of the 'ever not quite' must be carefully sought when trying to determine the relation between liberty and restraint in assent, if the life of reason is to be conducted responsibly.

James's work on religion cannot be properly understood apart from the foregoing conception of philosophy, and the epistemology of permissive and restraining influences upon belief which emerges from it. Neither theism nor atheism were more sacrosanct theoretically to James than any other theory. If the twists and turns of observation and inquiry move towards theism, then it is towards theism that one must travel; if they move towards atheism, then it is towards atheism that one's bearings must be set. The significance of the ever-not-quite-sufficient availability of empirical evidence in either case will have to be assessed with respect to both belief and doubt. Herein lies the challenge of epistemology, especially in matters as existentially influential theism.

The foregoing evidentialist depiction of James is foreign to the usual terms of reference within which his work on religion is approached by scholars. Throughout this century, he has been taken by most commentators to have recommended that in the case of certain beliefs, including religious ones, we set aside our usual allegiances to evidence, and allow personal influences to justify the adoption of a particular position. This impression seems to have been fostered especially by his famous essay *The Will to Believe*, a work which Richard Taylor conjectured is 'perhaps the most widely read essay on the rationality of faith ever written in English.'[7] From the presence of *The Will to Believe*, or sections of it, in many anthologies which address the epistemology of religious belief, one could conclude that Taylor's comments remain true now, more than 100 years after the essay appeared. It is not surprising, therefore, that the subjectivistic interpretations of James, which seem to be readily invited by that essay, continue to flourish.

On the face of it, James does seem to propose the position described above. In *The Will to Believe*, for example, he says that he is deploying a 'justification of faith' in the formation of beliefs which involve forced, momentous and live options, among which religion is to be included. He contrasts the class of beliefs involving faith with another class which, on account of its association with sensory experience and the practicalities of everyday life, is said to allow for indefinite delay pending the development of compelling evidence. In relation to this latter class he commends 'the attitude of sceptical balance.'[8] His contrast of these classes, and his advocacy of the involvement of 'passional nature' and volition in belief in the former, is what seems to have earned him the reputation, as Morton White put it graphically, as 'the patron saint of wishful thinking.'[9]

This reputation has been reinforced by many of James's writings, particularly those which defend pragmatism's appeals to the consequences of belief in the determination of truth. One of the consequences of theistic belief, James is widely held to have said, is a form of desirable personal edification. Bertrand Russell for example, among others, understood James to contend that theistic belief can be justifiably adopted and deemed to be true, on the strength of such desirable consequences.

Charges of wishful thinking are not the only ones levelled at James in connection with his position on belief, however. Even if it were the case that in the intellectual life one is sometimes forced to move ahead of what is justified evidentially, Russell and others argue, this ought to take the form not of belief but of hypothesis-adoption or some kind of gamble.[10]

There are two charges facing the common, subjectivist interpretations of James's work on belief, then, particularly in the area of religion: that he advocated wishful thinking, and confused belief and hypothesis-adoption. Both of these, as well as the interpretations of James to which they are closely tied, are untenable. They should be clearly exposed as such, and be set aside. This would make way for a clearer recognition of the merits of James's position, and a realignment of his work within contemporary epistemology and philosophy of religion.

An important step in this direction will be the establishment of the fact that at a number of pivotal locations in his work, in *The Will to Believe* for example, James was not concerned about propositions, theistic or otherwise, which are not *already* believed, or towards which there is not at least a propensity for belief. On such occasions he was not interested in the initiation of new beliefs, religious or otherwise. His concern was to assess the permissibility of continuing to believe under certain circumstances. I will show that in such central parts of his corpus, James was primarily interested in raising questions about the grounds for, and the significance of the continuation of belief.

This pivotal feature of James's position, especially in *The Will to Believe*, has been overlooked for decades because of the pervasive neglect of what he means by the notion of 'liveness.' A major component of my case will be to establish the centrality, in James's philosophy, of this idea of liveness. This will not only clarify his thought, but will bring him into line with current debates, among epistemologists and philosophers of religion, about what constitutes 'basic' beliefs.

A second major element of my case is related to the foregoing emphasis on liveness. Liveness matters because the abandonment of live propositions, particularly in religion, has significant epistemological, as well as personal, consequences. In the case of theism, in James's account, the belief state uniquely gives rise to certain important effects, including effects on intellectual inquiry itself. In particular, it occasions what James calls the 'strenuous mood,' a state which has intellectual as well as emotional components, as I will show. The abandonment of live theism has major consequences not only of a personal nature, then, but of an intellectual nature as well. An evidentialism which would essentially counsel the abandonment of live theism should be assessed carefully with a view to its implications in both these respects.

A major problem with James scholarship is that the strenuous mood, like liveness, has been widely neglected. This is particularly troublesome because the standard prudential interpretations of James, which take him to urge the adoption of religious belief on the basis of its edifying personal consequences, directly implicate the notion of the strenuous mood. It is under this heading that James developed his account of the consequences of religious belief. Commentators, however, have generally assumed that they already know what consequences follow from religious belief, and have read these into James's position. As I will show, however, James was, on many counts, deeply countercultural in his understanding of religion and its consequences. When this is taken into account, the longstanding prudential readings of his work, and the famous criticisms of him which are closely associated with such readings, prove to be untenable.

The second major aspect of my case, then, involves a close

inquiry into what exactly is involved in the strenuous mood. The considerations of liveness and the strenuous mood should be taken together if James's intentions regarding the relation between religious belief and its consequences are to be grasped properly. James is not defending the creation of beliefs principally on the basis of their personally edifying consequences, as is widely contended. He is proposing, rather, an alternative form of *evidentialism* – not a fideism – in response to widespread forms of evidentialism which he thought were insufficiently rigorous.

A third and overarching aspect of my case has to do with the context in which liveness and the strenuous mood stand in James's thought. Behind the charges about wishful thinking and the confusion of belief and hypothesis-adoption stands the widespread custom among commentators of isolating the role assigned by James to what he calls 'passional nature' from the larger setting within which that role actually functions in his thought as a whole. As I will show, such an isolation ignores the many constraints on subjectivity which are involved in James's epistemology. As my study unfolds, I will illustrate in detail how James contextualizes the role of the subject within the terms of reference of the complex unity of what he refers to as 'immediate experience.' Subject and world are *simultaneously* implicated in the constitution of experience and belief in such a way that subjective elements could not possibly possess the scope of influence often attributed to them by commentators.

It is this partnership of subject and world which moved James to defend belief rather than hypothesis-adoption in certain instances, including religious ones, and which precluded him from advancing the prudential argument so widely attributed to him. The subjective elements of the strenuous mood are inseparable from the intellectual elements of that mood, and both occur uniquely in the belief state, for reasons that I will spell out. The desirable subjective aspects of the strenuous mood cannot be appropriated in a prudentially self-interested way because they follow exclusively from a certain intellectual relationship with the world, a relationship, James says explicitly and unambiguously, which cannot be acquired at will.

My contention that liveness and the strenuous mood should be taken as major interpretive keys to James's philosophy of religion will involve a broader contextualization of these aspects of his position within the terms of reference of his multifaceted account of immediate experience. This contextualization will involve relating James's philosophy of religion, and his will to believe doctrine, to other aspects of his Radical Empiricism, including its tenacious methodological allegiances to observation and fact.

With these introductory comments in place, I shall turn my attention first to the broad terms of reference of James's philosophy of religion, for these will set the stage for developing the details of my position.

# 1

# The Woodpecker and the Grub

Certain distinctive patterns stand out in the critical reception of William James's thought over the last century. Prominent among these has been the accusation that his work is marred by the untenability of several features of pragmatism, and by some distinctive characteristics of his own form of pragmatism in particular. He confused the meaning of truth with the means of its pursuit, Bertrand Russell charged, for example, and the relationship between truth and utility which resulted from this confusion allowed him to accord to subjectivity a role in the formation of belief to which it is not entitled. Such a position has, in turn, thrown open the doors to wishful thinking, especially in the case of religion, and has allowed for the justification of religious belief on the basis of its edifying subjective effects.

This widespread and deeply entrenched understanding of James is not only inaccurate, but misses what is richest and most engaging in his thought. There is no doubt that he gave to subjectivity a major role in both his epistemology and his philosophy of religion. What has been widely neglected, however, is that he circumscribed the role of subjectivity in epistemology far more closely than is commonly recognized. Some preliminary generalizations about James's thought will help to set the stage for developing the details of my position in this respect.

The first generalization has to do with the nature of his philosophy as a whole. The way in which James integrates subjectivity into epistemology and philosophy of religion is indebted above all to the distinctive form of pragmatism which he came later in his life to call Radical Empiricism.[1] The radicalness of his empiricism lies above all in its insistence on the inclusion in philosophical reflection of all aspects of phenomena under philosophical scrutiny:

> To be radical, an empiricism must neither admit in its construc-tions any element that is not directly experienced, nor exclude from them any element that is directly experienced. For such a philosophy, *the relations that connect experiences must themselves be experienced relations, and any kind of relation experienced must be accounted as 'real' as anything else in the system.*[2]

The radicalness of this empiricism lies not only in its insis-tence on the inclusion of all available experiential data in philo-sophical reflection, but also in the seriousness with which it treats all the conceptual alternatives potentially applicable to a case at hand as well. Every alternative must be made repeatedly to 'dip' back, as James put it, into the everyday occurrence of the object in connection with which it is considered, in all the com-plexity of that object's concrete existence. Only such a relation-ship between the intellectual and the concrete would be able, in James's judgment, to hold at bay the 'clean-shaven' theories, which so often lay claim to comprehensiveness of understand-ing, but do so at the cost of underestimating the full depth and complexity of their subject.

The empirical and conceptual scope of radical empiricism puts heavy demands upon philosophical reflection. This is espe-cially the case with a subject as complex as religion. Radical Empiricism requires consideration of not only the many theo-logical and philosophical abstractions involved, but also the liv-ing phenomenon of religion itself, with which these abstractions are deeply and inextricably intertwined.

James diligently applies himself on both fronts. He attends carefully to the dominant idealist and scholastic theological trends of his day, for example, without neglecting the empirical research which emerges so clearly in *The Varieties of Religious Experience* and elsewhere. While some philosophers may disdain such empirical inquiry as 'slumming,' as Royce once called it, James is tenacious in his conviction that the detachment of philosophical reflection from the concrete domain in all its richness and detail is an open invitation to speculative, wishful thinking, and he wanted no part of it. As Louis Dupré observed, the rigour of Radical Empiricism's allegiance to concrete experience in the actual, multiform shape which it takes, left a distinctive mark on James's work in the area of religion:

> Most philosophical studies on religion of the recent past are totally outdated. In contrast with them the work of James, Royce, Hocking retains all its original freshness. The reason, I would guess, is that those authors, raised in the hard school of a pioneering country where a man had to find things out for himself, deemed it necessary to acquire experience before interpreting it. Nor did they, as the 'empiricists' of the past, restrict experience to sense perception and its interpretation. Those men let no one tell them what was, and what was not 'meaningful' as experience. Unfortunately, since then the 'radical' American empiricism has again been replaced by the narrow variety of which it had discarded the sensationalist dogmatism.[3]

The best place to enter the web-like results of Radical Empiricism's inquiries into religion is with a failure to which James confesses readily. He has been unable, he tells us, to find a common theological denominator among religions. 'The word "religion,"' he concludes, seems not to stand for 'any single principle or essence, but is rather a collective name.'[4] To what does this collective name refer? It refers to certain states of the subject, including feelings of seriousness, awe, and solemnity.

Such a portrayal of religion, however, is only one small part of a much broader view which includes many non-subjective considerations. James adds, for example, that such feelings do not stand alone, but are *responses* to a particular, albeit elusive object, 'a primal reality ... [which] the individual feels impelled to respond to solemnly and gravely.'[5] That religious feelings are aroused in response to a distinctive object impressed James in his empirical investigations, as did the many reports of a prominent noetic element in the relation between those feelings and their object. James found this noetic element, together with its object, so deeply implicated in religious subjectivity that such subjectivity, he concluded, cannot be properly understood apart from them. An account of his position which severs the affective from these metaphysical and noetic components, I will show, distorts his thought to the point of entirely misrepresenting his account of religion and subjectivity.

The philosophical significance of these metaphysical and noetic elements of religiosity will not emerge as it should, James predicts, in the absence of a vigorous reappraisal of the conventional practices often adopted by philosophers in deciding which human experiences have evidential significance. James is particularly concerned about the apparent arbitrariness with which these determinations are sometimes made. He observes, for example, the widespread propensity to ignore the many first-hand reports to the effect that religious subjectivity often involves a pronounced sense of what he calls a 'harmonious working relationship' with the world, an experience which is often regarded, in non-religious cases, as evidentially significant. He observes that at the same time, however, there exists a comparably widespread propensity to ignore the intrusion of subjective influences into purportedly disinterested forms of inquiry outside the domain of religion. Even Clifford's allegiance to philosophical disinterestedness, he points out for example, is deeply indebted to Clifford's own *sentiments*, not the least of which is his surpassing fear of error. James rightly calls for a vigorous reappraisal of such uneven practices.

The central role of subjectivity in James's account of religion also involves an allegiance to factuality which places many constraints on what may be justifiably believed. The notion that James advocated belief in what is personally attractive, without scrupulous regard for all factual considerations, and for the theological implications of these considerations, is utterly false. Any belief, religious or otherwise, James argues repeatedly, must be made to square with all the relevant facts about the world presently at our disposal. Among such facts, in the case of religion for example, is some version of natural selection.

Alongside theological claims to the sacredness of life, therefore, the incalculable sacrifice of life in the production of relatively few successful results must be acknowledged and accommodated. The world may be creation, but it is also a food chain. Nowhere does James allow that the personal utility of religious belief would in any way justify ignoring such facts. Notwithstanding his periodic jabs at things 'romish,' he has a strong sympathy with the spirit, at least, of traditional Roman Catholic natural theology's stubborn efforts, through the emphasis placed on Aquinas's five ways, to tie theological thought to the concrete natural order.

However subjectively appealing religion may be, James warned, it could not ignore the many major obstacles created by our unfolding understanding of the facts about the world. Previous generations of believers had seen the world predominantly in terms of design, and had constructed their arguments accordingly. Under Darwin's tutelage, however, the world has increasingly come to be seen in terms of natural selection, in terms, that is, of the propensity of 'chance-happenings to bring forth "fit" results if only they have time to add themselves together' (emphasis added).[6]

This shift of perspective, James points out, cannot be accommodated simply by amending traditional argumentation to include evolution as an instrument of divine creative activity. A successful integration of evolution into natural theology must come more fully to terms with the complexity of the evolutionary process itself, and this, he anticipated, would be difficult. After Darwin, a mechanism of extraordinary scope has entered the picture between the creator and world. That mechanism has proven to be 'so vast as to be incomprehensible to us humans,'[7] in James's judgment, and it will greatly impede the efforts of generations to come to grasp, through the natural order, the nature of a cosmic mind,[8] if there is one.

If we genuinely honour the facts presently within our grasp, James concludes it is a 'strange mixture of goods and evils that we find'[9] in the world. A strange mixture it is indeed. 'To the grub under the bark,' he observes, 'the exquisite fitness of the woodpecker's organism to extract him would certainly argue a diabolical designer.'[10] Much natural and philosophical theology over the centuries has been done by individuals who have been privileged culturally, by church or academy, to be the intellectual woodpeckers of their time. Now, however, as more grubs have their say, the strangeness of the mixture of goods and evils that we call the world is emerging more prominently. James would have celebrated this. It is, he would have said, the triumph of the oft-neglected facts which reside in the concrete *'particulars'* of the world, particulars which are so often conveniently ignored by theorists, religious or anti-religious, but sought out tirelessly by Radical Empiricism.

While James wonders aloud about the prospects of rising to the philosophical challenges created by such facts, he never flags in his allegiance to a scrupulous consultation of the natural order in its entirety and its details, when exploring religion. 'We can study our God only by studying his Creation,'[11] he insists, and can do so above all by studying 'nature's particulars.'[12] Only great diligence in attending to all particulars will prevent theory from lapsing into wishful thinking, and such diligence is the hallmark of Radical Empiricism. The lessons of the grub are no less significant than the lessons of the woodpecker, and the real significance of the one cannot be grasped fully apart from the significance of the other.

The central role that subjectivity plays in James's understanding of religion is constrained by not only the metaphysical, noetic, evidential and factual elements set out in the foregoing pages, but also by discursive and theological ones as well. The subjective states he found so widespread among religious persons cannot ultimately be kept separate from metaphysical questions about the nature of the universe, and the propositional responses to which such questions give rise. 'We must ... pass beyond the point of view of merely subjective utility' when it comes to religion, he says as his position unfolds in the *Varieties*, 'and make inquiry into the intellectual content itself.'[13]

Such intellectual content is expressed in what James calls 'overbeliefs.' While overbeliefs are subject to ongoing revision, they are not, on that account, of marginal significance only. They are, he insists, 'essential to [the] ... individual's religion; –

which is as much as to say that over-beliefs in various directions are absolutely indispensable.'[14] He adds, moreover, that the kinds of questions which give rise to overbeliefs cannot be satisfactorily responded to with hermeneutical answers:[15]

Religion, in her fullest exercise of function, is not a mere illumination of facts already elsewhere given, not a mere passion, like love, which views things in a rosier light. It is indeed that, as we have seen abundantly. But it is something more, namely, a postulator of new *facts* as well. The world interpreted religiously is not the materialistic world over again, with an altered expression; it must have, over and above the altered expression, a *natural constitution* different at some point from that which a materialistic world would have. It must be such that different events can be expected in it, different conduct must be required.[16]

Taking these assertions by James into account, and the overall position that has emerged so far, I propose that his conception of the religious state is better construed on the model which Rudolph Otto used in *The Idea of the Holy.*[17] According to the latter, religion is an irreducibly *dialectical* phenomenon. One element of this dialectic, the living subject, is not ultimately separable from its discursive counterpart, and particularly the metaphysical and cognitive elements of that counterpart. Human beings may for a time be able to force the subjective and discursive aspects of religion apart, but the resulting fragmentation yields only subjectivistic fanaticism or dry theological intellectualism, both of which destroy religion in the end.

While James emphasizes subjectivity in his account of religion, then, it is a notion of subjectivity that is profoundly enriched by his conception of the wide range of relationships among subjective and non-subjective influences which constitute immediate experience as a whole.

The room for subjective influence in religious belief diminishes a good deal when we consider James's understanding of the nature of religion from the point of view of his ethical thought. 'If you wish to grasp her [religion's] essence, you must look to the feeling and the conduct as being the more constant elements' (emphasis added).[18] The understanding of religion which emerges from James's scrutiny of such conduct is deeply at odds with the understanding of religion presupposed by most interpretations and criticisms of his philosophy of religion. We can better appreciate this contrast by beginning with some preliminary observations about the nature of the divine, as James understands it.

While the plurality of religions makes it difficult to define the nature of the divine, James concedes, the indispensability of overbeliefs in this area requires that certain theological basics are put in place. Among such basics, the term God, he says, will serve as 'the natural appellation, for us Christians at least, for the supreme reality.'[19] In addition, however, the divine should also be considered to be 'finite, either in power or in knowledge, or in both at once.'[20]

Since an assertion of divine limitation seems to clash with the tradition of much Christianity, it will appear doubly odd to find James arguing that the principal reason for adopting such a view is its conventionality. Predicating finitude of the divine, he insists nevertheless, accords with 'the terms in which common men have usually carried on their active commerce with God.'[21] Surely, however, the major theological creeds which are used so widely among Christian believers have much to say about divine infinitude and omnipotence. They seem to often say such things, moreover, in unabashedly metaphysical terms, and appear to have been understood by generations of believers and scholars in precisely such terms. Why, then, would James claim that his assertion of divine finitude commends itself on account of its accord with conventional religious belief?

James's reasons for holding this position are closely related to his stipulation that we need to attend, in this matter, to religious peoples' 'active commerce with God.' The concept of divinity in which he is interested, in other words, is the concept which is implicit in religious behaviour, including worship and spirituality. What do we find in such behaviour? For one thing, the language involved is overwhelmingly the language of narrative, prayer, liturgy, song, and so forth. It is deeply analogical and metaphorical, and rarely explicitly metaphysical. The divine is the mysterious providential guide in the Sinai desert, the just judge of the nations, the good shepherd, the father of the prodigal son, the mother hen longing to gather her chicks, the patron of the outcast, widow and orphan, and so on. This is no Aristotelian Unmoved Mover, but a being very much moved, by concrete events, to mercy or pity, to moral indignation or to judgment.[22]

The focus of divine involvement, as described in the narratives and metaphors used in actual religious practice, rather than just in technical philosophical theology, has to do primarily with *saving*, saving an individual, a people, a land, or a national heritage. It has to do with 'plucking from harm's way,' as the Hebrew terminology describes it. It rarely involves metaphysical speculation, although it may imply and shed light on important philosophical matters. James recognizes that religion is fundamentally soteriological rather than speculative in character. 'There is a certain uniform deliverance in which religions all appear to meet. It consists of two parts: 1. An uneasiness; and 2. Its solution. 1. The uneasiness, reduced to its simplest terms, is a sense that there is *something wrong about us* as we naturally stand. The solution is a sense that *we are saved from the wrongness* by making proper connection with the higher powers.'[23]

James also recognizes that such a connection with higher powers involves a crucial *reciprocity*. The moral beliefs, ascetic practices and spiritual self-expectations of the large majority of religious people in the major monotheisms of the world manifest at every turn the assumption that reciprocal collaboration with the divine is not merely helpful but somehow also indispensable in the pursuit of the welfare of both humans and the earth.

Such indispensability, James argues, must involve some limitation of the divine. Contemporary theodicists as diverse in their views on this subject as John Hick, Brian Davies, and Louis Dupré, may disagree about the metaphysical implications of reciprocity between free humans and a sovereign deity, but they agree that there are serious philosophical problems in this area. These problems are the terms of reference within which James's position on divine finitude should be understood.

What is most important for our present purposes, however, is not how this particular issue of James's position vis à vis contemporary theodicy plays out in detail, but the impact of his understanding of God on his view of religion. The major impact here is the magnification of moral responsibility which falls to human beings for the welfare of themselves and their world. For James, humans play an indispensable role in world-making and therefore the future of the world is still undecided. The survival and well-being of the world, according to such a 'melioristic' position, is neither inevitable nor impossible.[24] It is a fundamentally historical matter which has yet to unfold in its entirety.

Such a view contrasts with what James calls a 'rationalist' position which provides 'a guarantee that the upshot shall be good. Taken in this way, the absolute makes all good things certain, and all bad things impossible (in the eternal, namely), and may be said to transmute the entire category of possibility into categories more secure.'[25] The powerful appeal of such an idealist position lies in its responsiveness to the 'need of an eternal moral order' among human beings, a need which 'is one of the deepest needs of our breast.'[26] Idealist thought caters to this need, offering 'the assurance that however disturbed the surface may be, at bottom all is well with the cosmos – central peace abiding at the heart of endless agitation.'[27] In all this, James observes, such thought is deeply satisfying.

James, however, is certainly not satisfied! No matter how *personally* attractive such a view may be to the 'deepest needs of our breast,' it achieves its appeal only by 'spurning the dust' of the particulars of life. 'It keeps no connexion whatever with concreteness;'[28] it 'remains supremely indifferent to what the particular facts in our world actually are.'[29] His response is clear. 'Far be it from me to deny the majesty of this conception, or its capacity to yield religious comfort to a most respectable class of minds.'[30] However, 'from the human point of view, no one can pretend that it doesn't suffer from the faults of remoteness and abstractness. It is eminently a product of what I have ventured to call the rationalist temper. It disdains empiricism's needs. It substitutes a pallid outline for the real world's richness.'[31]

Human beings may want assurance, but such assurance, insists Radical Empiricism, can never be seized in contravention of the facts which are involved in 'the real world's richness,' for good or ill. Nor can assurance be seized without responding coherently to difficult philosophical questions raised by idealist theology, especially in its eschatological forms. Even if there were a final divine intervention which would guarantee a good end to the world, what exactly would be the relation between that final state of affairs, and the states of affairs which have preceded it in the history of the world? 'All tears will be dried,' it is often responded; 'all will be made well.' Such consoling words, however personally edifying, are beside the point. They are words of compensation. However, compensation does not necessarily explain or justify, much less undo, the often tragic, actual historical events through which the lives of individual human beings over the ages are constituted.

At bottom, then, in its emphasis on eschatology or a parallel supra-historical domain, idealist thought essentially 'represents the deepest reality of the world as static and without history.'[32] It rejects 'the finite world of change and striving.'[33] For James, however, if the world and those who inhabit it are constituted in and through change and striving, then religion calls for a vigorous moral engagement with the world, whatever the personal cost. This engagement James calls the 'strenuous mood,' a central but, as I indicated in my Introduction, neglected part of his philosophy of religion which will play a major role in this book. The strenuous mood is a disposition towards the world aroused by the recognition that without vigorous human collaboration with the divine, often involving costly self-sacrifice, the world as we wish it to be will never exist. The strenuous mood is a demanding disposition which emerges in response to a recognition of the deeply historical character of all existence.

It is here that we find the ethical heart of religion, as James sees it:

Suppose that the world's author put the case to you before creation, saying: 'I am going to make a world not certain to be saved, a world the perfection of which shall be conditional merely, the condition being that each several agent does its own 'level best.' I offer you the chance of taking part in such a world. Its safety, you see, is unwarranted. It is a real adventure, with real danger, yet it may win through. It is a social scheme of cooperative work genuinely to be done. Will you join the procession? Will you trust yourself and trust the other agents enough to face the risk?[34]

This, for James, is the question which religion addresses to all people. The risk is real, and many of the consequences of an affirmative response will be painful.

If pragmatism were as wedded to self-interest as Russell and many others have said that it is, this is not the kind of religiosity we would expect to find it advocate. Russell and most critics, however, have not paid attention to the details of James's understanding of religion and the strenuous mood. They have assumed that religion provides a secure and optimistic frame of mind and the 'moral holiday,' as James calls it, which arises from such optimism. James rejects this, however, as shamelessly catering to the longings of the human heart rather than to the facts of the world as revealed in its particulars. A religiosity which is adopted for the sake only of such solace, in James's view, is fraudulent. Authentic religion is religion which squares with the facts of the world and is 'willing to take the universe to be really dangerous and adventurous, without therefore backing out and crying "no play."'[35]

There are elements of actual religious practice which support James's position in the foregoing respects, however unconventional some of the theology involved in it may appear. The demand for reparation where possible as a precondition of divine forgiveness, according to Roman Catholicism for example, reflects such a view. Such practices are, in turn, deeply rooted in the imagery of the opening chapters of the book of *Genesis* to which these communities look for their foundational religious vision. Those chapters portray the human being as deputed by the Creator, who is depicted in monarchical imagery, to carry out the divine will in an *ongoing historical process* of creation. The story of the Fall is not about sex, law, or deceit, but the refusal or abuse of fiduciary responsibility.

Only a deeply historical understanding of the world and religion which takes present human actions and their concrete effects on the real world seriously squares with such religious literature. James's position is, on many points, highly congruent with the views of these communities. The main point for present purposes, however, is that prudential interpretations of James which assume the wholesale desirability of the religious state are seriously incongruent with his account of the strenuous mood and religious life in general.

So far I have observed a number of ways in which the central role of subjectivity in James's philosophy of religion is circumscribed by various elements. It might be asked at this point in what way the position which has emerged is a form of pragmatism at all. How do the volitional, practical and personal influences usually associated with pragmatism figure in all this? Is there not still a 'leap' which has to be made beyond available evidence, and even beyond the restraining influence of the factors described up to this point? Would not such a leap still come down to a fundamentally personal choice which is open to the criticisms traditionally levelled at James for having advocated the adoption of belief on subjective, rather than evidential grounds?

In my Introduction I said that there were two aspects of the reception of James which I intended to address. The first has to do with the claim that James was commending the creation of religious belief. The second has to do with the role of subjectivity in this connection. Both issues are implicated in a proper understanding of pragmatism.

With respect to the first, I indicated that James is not interested in commending the creation of religious belief at all. It is not possible, he says, for a human being to create a new belief, no matter how pragmatically appealing its possession may be; one can only build upon belief or a propensity to believe already in existence. 'We cannot create a belief out of whole cloth,'[36] he says clearly in the *Varieties*, and elsewhere he plainly rejects pretension to belief.[37] The famous 'will to believe' doctrine has nothing to do with willing into existence a new belief, religious or otherwise. James is principally interested in what we should do about existing forms of belief, rather than the creation of new beliefs.

An important key to his thought in this respect is his comment in the *Varieties* that in his time religious belief was increasingly stigmatized as intellectually irresponsible. 'The current of thought in academic circles runs against me, and I feel like a man who must set his back against an open door quickly if he does not wish to see it closed and locked.'[38] He was convinced that the growing presumption of atheism was philosophically unsound, and one of his main aims was to challenge it. What he commends is the entitlement to maintain an existing belief or propensity to believe in the face of this cultural attack. Many of his arguments which have been construed as invitations to create religious belief, in other words, are actually defences of existing beliefs from cultural attack.

The issue that concerns James above all, then, particularly in his will to believe doctrine, is what would constitute intellectually responsible behaviour towards certain existing beliefs, including religious ones which, while not entirely conclusive evidentially, are nonetheless generally congruent with the many constraints on subjectivity laid out so far in this chapter. This concern is far from the focal point of stereotypes of James which portray him as contending that, in cases of insufficient evidence, purely subjective influences may legitimately seize the field and dominate the determination of belief.

Such stereotypes are seriously misleading, although their tenacity and longevity are not surprising. James's respect for the gradualness with which the truth about the world unfolds through human inquiry over the ages is reminiscent of Kierkegaard's assessment of the same process, and some features of James's response to this phenomenon are no less reminiscent of Kierkegaard's fideism. That is, while human inquiry as such may proceed indefinitely through its long history of approximations, James and Kierkegaard both agree, an individual human being's inquiries transpire within the much shorter confines of a single, brief life. Because such a life is constituted by the succession of its individual days and decisions, suspension of judgment on important metaphysical matters leaves its mark permanently and irreversibly on each life. There is a profound difference between the human community and the individual in this respect, therefore, a difference which creates serious practical problems for the individual. On what basis *is* one to give shape, possibly religious shape, to such a brief life?

James's pragmatism appears at first fideistic in its response to this question, for a distinctive personal element moves prominently to the fore. 'Pending the slow answer from facts' in the ongoing scrutiny of a very complicated concrete world, James says, we should note that 'any one who insists that there *is* a designer and who is sure he is a divine one, gets a certain pragmatic benefit from the term.'[39] It is quite clear, however, that 'a certain pragmatic benefit,' Russell rightly pointed out, can be derived from innumerable patent falsehoods. Of course I will be happier if I believe I have unlimited material resources rather than the pile of bills stacked on my desk. James has been pilloried for supposedly neglecting this obvious point by counselling the adoption of beliefs on the basis of their edifying personal effects.

In fact, however, James does not propose such a crassly pragmatic position. He is vigilant in his allegiance to Radical Empiricism's demand that *all* relevant data and all possible conceptual alternatives be involved alongside subjective influences in responding to the challenge of life's brevity. In connection with religion he directs us, in the spirit of Radical Empiricism, to be 'willing to take anything, to follow either logic or the senses, and to count the humblest and most personal experiences. She will count mystical experiences if they have practical consequences. She will take a God who lives in the very dirt of private fact – if that should seem a likely place to find him.'[40]

The attention of some readers may be drawn to the term '*anything*' here, which James uses to describe what is admissible in the justification of religious belief. This terminology may suggest an indiscriminateness in the process of justification which has been associated with James's thought for a long time. When he says 'anything' in this connection, however, James means not anything *whatsoever* which happens to suit the individual's personal tastes, but *everything*, from the deliverances of sense experience and logical analysis, to the most mundane elements of everyday life, which many theorists choose to ignore.

Here I return to the theme of my opening comments in this chapter and the Introduction, about Radical Empiricism's tenacious allegiance to the entirety of experience, to the perspective of the grub as well as that of the woodpecker. It is accurate to say that for James the 'only test of probable truth is what works best in the way of leading us.' To this he adds, however, that workability has to do with 'what fits *every* part of life best and combines with the *collectivity* of experience's demands, *nothing* being omitted' (emphasis added).[41] When he talks about 'what fits every part of life best,' he means exactly what he says: *every* part, theoretical as well as practical, impersonal as well as personal. He repeats himself on this matter often, and does so explicitly in connection with religion. 'The truth of "God" has to run the gauntlet of *all* our other truths. It is on trial by them and they on trial by it.'[42]

Fair enough, one might respond. If this can be shown in detail, which I will do in this book, then perhaps we must concede that the longstanding stereotypes about James's account of the role of subjectivity in religion should be revised. Even if this is so, however, a serious problem remains. All restraints on subjectivity still do not vindicate religious belief decisively, from an evidential point of view. What, then, entitles one to hold a belief which moves beyond such restraints on subjectivity, and which credits the aforementioned personal benefits of religious belief with any justificatory significance at all?

The problem with this all-too-familiar question is that whether or not to *adopt* belief in the face of insufficient evidence is not the point. The real question is: what would constitute responsible behaviour towards religious belief which *already* exists, and which seems deeply reasonable to many of those who embrace it? James, in other words, is not interested in prompting us to check the evidence and *then* to will ourselves into adopting a new belief which surpasses such evidence, but which brings distinctive personal rewards. The issue with which he is preoccupied, rather, is whether there are solid grounds for calling for the *abandonment* of certain existing beliefs or propensities to believe which persist in the constellation of constraints furnished by the many influences which have been outlined so far in this chapter.

What James concludes in this matter is that the conventional Clifford-like view, which sees intellectual responsibility as calling for the abandonment of such beliefs, is wrong. When we examine closely the many dimensions of those beliefs, James holds, we come to see that the call to abandon them, in the name of intellectual integrity, is a cultural eccentricity which is itself evidentially dubious. Religious belief, to use current terminology, can be construed as a properly *basic* belief. The nature of being properly basic, in James's account, is particularly complex and interesting, and a clarification of it can make a significant contribution to the current debate about epistemically basic beliefs.

James's core position, I contend, is at the heart of *The Will to Believe*, and is widely reflected elsewhere in his corpus. The failure of previous literature on James to do justice to it is, to a significant degree, a function of the almost universal neglect of one feature of James's thought, which will be the centrepiece of the next chapter. When James's position on the nature of 'liveness' is clarified, it will be apparent that his philosophical place is not among the fideists, with whom he is often associated, but with those philosophers who, in substantial numbers today, argue against the modern presumption of atheism, and do so on the grounds of claims about the epistemically basic character of religious belief.

Is there not still a 'leap' of some kind advocated by James, I asked at the beginning of the foregoing digression, a leap beyond available evidence and the restraining influences on subjectivity described in this chapter? Perhaps there is a leap. The magnitude and nature of it, however, must be determined with great care on the basis of a close analysis of James's position. This has not generally been done in past analyses of James's philosophy of religion, in my judgment, but is what I will endeavour to do.

It is time now, in the development of my case, to turn from

the generalities of this opening chapter, to more focused considerations. I will begin with *The Will to Believe*, and then show the congruence between that work and other parts of James's corpus. The position that will emerge is not the one that most commentators attribute to James. James, in my view, endorses neither wishful thinking nor any of the other subjectivistic proposals attributed to him over the decades. His epistemology is wonderfully complex and involves internalist, externalist, pragmatic, coherentist, and other elements. It deserves close attention today in the climate of debate about what is constitutive of epistemically basic beliefs, especially in the case of religion.

# 2

## *The Will to Believe*

*The Will to Believe* was first presented by James to the Philosophical Clubs of Brown and Yale Universities in 1896. It was subsequently published in *New World* in 1896,[1] then reprinted in 1897[2] and 1917.[3] The general pattern of his argument in the essay emerges in a review by James of *The Unseen Universe* by P.G. Tait in 1875.[4] In that review, James speaks about a 'duty' to believe, holding that belief in a transcendent realm was not only permissible but something which one may be duty-bound to hold if it would, for the believer, be a source of commendable action or peace of mind. In the review of Tait's work James characterizes the abdication of such a duty to hold salutary beliefs as a residual consequence of overextended '"scientific" scruples.' His choice of duty terminology in the review appears to have had its origins in his contact with the work of Charles Renouvier, to whom James announced his indebtedness at the outset of his presentation of *The Will to Believe*.

James seems gradually to have drifted away from the influence of Renouvier, however, and away also from a duty-to-believe position.[5] The influence of Chauncey Wright, the Cambridge philosopher and James's personal friend, was instrumental in this regard. Despite their philosophical agreement on a number of issues Wright was markedly antagonistic towards James's review in the *Nation*. In a letter to Grace Norton in July of 1875 Wright reported a conversation that he had with James about the offending passages.[6] Wright had told James that the

*Nation* account, as it stood, appeared to undermine the importance of evidence in the formation of beliefs, an impression which James later said that he had not intended to give. As a result of the conversation with Wright, James abandoned duty terminology. As Wright put it 'he agreed that attention to all accessible evidence was the only duty involved in belief.'[7] The accuracy of Wright's report that James had decided to abandon duty terminology is borne out by the fact that the term is not used again by James to describe his position after 1875.[8]

While James abandoned duty terminology, he retained a variety of other terms over the years to describe his position, a position which, as James Wernham has shown, did not really change in its basic substance as a result of the discussions with Wright. In a letter to Mark Baldwin in 1899 concerning criticisms of *The Will to Believe* by Dickinson Miller, James expressed the belated wish that he had entitled his essay 'a defense of faith, or words to that effect.'[9] In another letter in 1901 he again expressed regret for having opted for *The Will to Believe* title, proposing in its place 'Critique of Pure Faith' as a possible improvement.[10] It is in terms, however, of a 'right' or a 'will' to believe, in the end, that James seems ultimately to have found himself best able to convey his position. He showed a preference for the former, 'right,' as late as 1904 when he wrote to L.T. Hobhouse that his essay should have been entitled 'The *Right* to Believe,'[11] a preference borne out by Dickinson Miller who also reports that James had expressed an attraction to the term.[12]

In general, then, the position which James was attempting to put forward in *The Will to Believe* was a position which developed publically between the 1875 review in the *Nation*, and later correspondence following the essay's publication. That position seems to have centred on the notion of a 'right' and a 'will,' rather than a 'duty,' having to do with certain sorts of beliefs under particular circumstances. Later comments to the effect that a better title would have been 'a defense of faith, or words to that effect' echo the opening passages of the essay as we now have it according to which its focus is on a defence of 'a believing attitude in religious matters.'[13]

Most secondary literature on *The Will to Believe* indicates that

James gave the impression of having promoted a questionable intrusion of personal influences into the intellectual domain. This body of work is characterized by 'mainly hostile criticisms,'[14] principally the charge that James was commending wishful thinking. Both Peirce and Dewey, for example, were critical of *The Will to Believe* on this count. 'I thought your *Will to Believe* was a very exaggerated utterance, such as injures a serious man very much,'[15] complained Pierce, and Dewey regretted what he thought had been James's effort to identify too closely *any* good which might accrue from a proposition, with the truth of such a proposition. Dewey was dismayed by James's apparent suggestion that the short-term satisfaction of emotional and other subjective states ought to have a major if not definitive role in the determination of truth, in the absence of persuasive evidence. Peirce would have concurred with Dewey's insistence that the only form of satisfaction which is directly pertinent to determining truth is the satisfaction of one's expectations regarding the outcome of experiment.[16]

Comparable concerns in more recent literature are typified by John Hick's analyses.[17] James's position, Hick argues, takes Pascal's Wager, and the wager's depiction of belief as 'a game of chance,' as its 'pilot scheme.'[18] One therefore finds an 'essentially sporting nature ... [in his] attitude to these ultimate issues of belief.'[19] While conceding that James's conception of God may involve more benevolence than Pascal's 'touchy eastern potentate,' James's argument is otherwise identical to Pascal's, Hick contends, and as Pascal's prudent gamble has been so offensive to many philosophers for its apparent self-serving character, so the belief advocated by James is no less offensive. Such belief entails 'treating as certain a proposition which you know (or believe) is not certain,'[20] and doing so for purposes of personal benefit. James essentially advocates wishful thinking,[21] that is, approves of assent to any non-demonstrably false proposition 'which ... might be advantageous to us.'[22] In essence, charges Hick:

> is he not saying that since the truth is unknown to us we may believe what we like and that while we are about it we had better

believe what we like most? This is certainly unjust to James's intention; but is it unjust to the logic of his argument? I do not see that it is: and I therefore regard James's theory as open to refutation by a *reductio ad absurdum*.[23]

Bertrand Russell had kindred reservations about James's position, as I indicated above. He was particularly concerned about pragmatic epistemology's consequence-oriented understanding of belief, especially with regard to theism in which 'the proposition in question has an emotional interest on its own account.'[24] A factually false proposition in such cases could be emotionally rewarding, Russell argued, and could 'work' in such a way that it could be deemed to be true by pragmatic standards. In essence, then, Russell charged, in the wishful-thinking vein, James ends up being 'prepared to advocate any doctrine which tends to make people virtuous and happy; if it does so, it is "true" in the sense in which he uses that word.'[25]

While the most common charge against *The Will to Believe* has involved wishful thinking, some commentators have also criticized its apparent misunderstanding of the relation between belief and hypothesis-adoption. Foreshadowing these concerns, Mark Baldwin, for example, argued in 1899 that a 'more-or-less-vaguely-grounded-hypothesis may rightly be an object of genuine belief,' but that it was a 'voluntary-guessing-or-throwing-of-dice under the impulse of passion, freedom, and the like,' which was to be found in *The Will to Believe*. Such a guess is a 'deliberate pretension to belief, to knowledge; it is deliberate make-believe, for personal advantage, and so is essentially immoral when employed for social purposes. Also essentially bad in the private life, for it loosens the moorings of real conviction in the world of evidence.'[26]

Bertrand Russell's criticisms of James regarding belief and hypothesis-adoption were more focussed than Baldwin's. James's position was seriously compromised, Russell charged, by borrowing heavily from a model of scientific hypothesis-adoption from which, James had failed to recognize, 'belief is absent.'[27] James, in commending belief in what he himself called the religious 'hypothesis,' had essentially proposed an understanding of belief modelled on a scientific form of inquiry which involves no belief but only hypothesis-adoption.

Russell's concerns with respect to hypothesis-adoption and belief have recently been taken up by James Wernham, but have been given a distinctive twist. There are more problems than Russell anticipated in James's authorization for adopting belief rather than an hypothesis in advance of appropriate evidential justification, Wernham argues. For Wernham, theism cannot function even hypothetically, for reasons I will outline later, and certainly need not be believed in order to be embraced. When one sorts through the various dimensions of James's errors in this area, according to Wernham's 'heretical' analysis, *The Will to Believe* turns out to be about neither belief, as scholarly orthodoxy has traditionally held,[28] nor hypothesis-adoption. Rather, it is about an obligation which 'is prudential, not moral,'[29] to undertake a 'pure' gamble on theism.

Wernham's criticisms of James regarding a confusion of belief and hypothesis-adoption give a current voice to the longstanding prudential interpretation of *The Will to Believe*. According to this traditional view, James authorized the adoption of theism in order prudentially to avail oneself of the personal benefits which accrue from holding such a belief, a position which once again, in our own time, raises the spectre of wishful thinking.

Dickinson Miller stands apart among commentators for not only recognizing potential problems in James's position regarding wishful thinking and the relation between belief and hypothesis-adoption, but connecting these with what James says about the liveness of certain options and propositions in *The Will to Believe*. James's position, Miller thought, rested on a 'deep confusion between belief and will,' and a related, erroneous application of the notion of 'hypothesis' to cases of religious belief.[30] 'In proportion ... as it [a proposition] is literally a hypothesis it is not a belief,' claimed Miller, and insofar as it is not a belief, its status can be in no way affected by volition but only by further evidence which may in turn support claims to its probable truth and entitlement to assent.[31] On the other hand, 'in proportion as it [a proposition] is actually a belief it is not a hypothesis.'[32] Volition is once again excluded, for a belief 'is not a voluntary conception; it is precisely an involuntary conception;'[33] one believes certain things because they impose themselves on the believer 'of their own accord, without any interference from our will ... If *we* arrange them according to our wish, that is not belief but imagination.'[34] In sum, for Miller, 'so far from faith being synonymous with working-hypothesis the two ideas are mutually exclusive.'[35]

Further exacerbating the liabilities in James's position with respect to belief and hypothesis-adoption, in Miller's view, was the nebulousness of James's account of truth. Truth, for James, is not 'a thing largely charted, largely based on definite principles of thinking.' It is, rather, 'an *aperçu*, a piercing glance of insight, a thing unique in each case, which often, and especially in the highest cases, could not be brought to book or turned into argument.'[36] If truth were ultimately about such insight, Miller objects, then the utility of the many logical and analytic tools normally used to distinguish probability from desirability would be hopelessly compromised, making way for the wholesale intrusion of self-interest. The nebulousness of James's procedures which are proposed in lieu of such conventional analytic tools leaves James's readers in the dark regarding just how his tests 'are tests of truth, how they are experimental, how they prove the point, how far they prove it, and how long they take to prove it.'[37] The fallibility of conventional procedures to which James is fond of calling attention, Miller protests, does not overturn the fact that even 'where logic is not a test of certain truth, it is very frequently a signal test of probability.'[38] Miller concluded, in line with much secondary literature on the essay, that 'the intervention of "our passional nature," of which James approves, is that which chiefly interferes, in all human beings, with good and trustworthy judgement,'[39] and he remained convinced over many years that '"the will to believe" is the will to deceive oneself; it is the will to regard something as true which is doubtful.'[40]

In Miller's case, however, such familiar charges were rooted in a distinctively clear-sighted recognition of the importance of *liveness* in James's position. James's 'irresponsible'[41] disregard for conventional criteria of truth, and for the 'slowly gathered and painstaking processes that have evinced themselves the surest reliance of our race,'[42] had led to a confusion of the personal desirability of a proposition with its argumentatively and evidentially-based probability, a confusion which stood squarely at the heart of James's account of liveness. James, Miller charged, 'declines to discriminate ... [probability] from such inducements to belief as attractions, values, appeals to desire. Probability and desirability alike he calls "liveliness".'[43] Not only had James 'declined' to discriminate probability from desire in the case of liveness, Miller also recognized, he had claimed as well that it is sometimes the case that 'amongst the inducements to belief we *cannot* separate probability from desirability' (emphasis added).[44] This point will turn out to be a central one as my study unfolds, for it is directly related to the way in which James understood subject and world to be simultaneously implicated in the constitution of experience.[45]

The patterns of analysis of *The Will to Believe* set out above exist against the background of James's protest that he had been improperly understood, and against the background of support, by a minority of commentators, of James's contentions to this effect. Mark Baldwin, James claimed, for example, had been attacking a 'man of straw,'[46] while F.H. Bradley and A.E. Taylor failed dismally to grasp his intentions.[47] In 1904 James wrote to L.T. Hobhouse, who had published a critique of *The Will to Believe* that year, disclaiming the position attributed to him by Hobhouse, and claiming that Hobhouse's own position was the one that he, James, had in fact intended to propose.[48] Hobhouse had held that feeling has a legitimate role in the formation of belief because it is often a compelling 'forerunner of thought.' James insists that his own advocacy of a place for feeling in the life of the intellect was, like Hobhouse's, based upon its link with reasoning, a link which James had tried, he said, to protect.[49]

Such protests by James against his critics are also reflected in his response to an opponent from the fideistic end of the religious spectrum. In March 1897 James received a letter from a strongly evangelical fideist, John Chapman, who criticized him for having recommended that any evidential support at all be sought for religious belief. While diplomatically indulgent of

Chapman, James rejected Chapman's fideism, arguing that there must be an intellectual root for religious belief.[50]

The contention that James had been misunderstood has been advanced as well by philosophers other than James himself. Gail Kennedy has argued this, for example, based in part on his analysis of exchanges between James and Dewey. Dewey saw James, he argues, as having come to place too much weight on personal satisfaction in the determination of meaning and truth, and both Dewey and Peirce had proposed that only '*that* satisfaction which arises when the idea as working hypothesis or tentative method is applied to prior existences in such a way as to fulfil what it intends' is a satisfaction which ought to influence judgments regarding truth or falsity.[51] What is notable, Kennedy points out, is that James agreed with Dewey on this in a letter in 1907.[52]

Kennedy's thesis is that Dewey and Peirce had misunderstood James. Peirce and Dewey, assuming a scientific context, thought about long term truth-seeking from a 'standard observer' point of view, allowing for repeated trial and error and an ongoing assessment of the results of such trial and error. James would have agreed with what they had to say on this count, he thinks. James's question, however, had been a different one; his was a question about the dynamics of the short-run situation in which a decision must be taken without the luxury of an extended testing process. 'James did not intend to alter Peirce's criteria of verification, he merely intended to extend their application' to situations which had not formerly been taken into account.[53]

James, Dewey, and Peirce, in other words, according to Kennedy, had been arguing at cross purposes, unaware that they were applying essentially the same pragmatic method to significantly different circumstances. 'In making James's extension [of the views of Dewey and Peirce to the short term] there is no need ... to alter the *method*.'[54] Rather, the various elements involved in that method – verification, sense experience, desire etc. – operate somewhat differently. The verificatory moves further into the background and the volitional moves more prominently into the foreground.

There are a number of other commentators who have also held that James had been misunderstood, although they differ in their interpretations of the exact form which this misunderstanding has taken. Madden, for example, is convinced that 'James was genuinely misunderstood in his will-to-believe doctrine,'[55] and that it is 'a gross misreading to hold that James advocated believing whatever one wants if so doing makes one happy or has any need-fulfilling results.'[56]

> It is not that Renouvier or James thought that affective and volitional elements determine decisions beyond the capacity of the individual to control – far from it, since their view is not a variation on scepticism or sociology-of-knowledge viewpoints – but rather that affective and volitional elements have a legitimate epistemic role to play in reaching certain decisions.[57]

The root of this misreading of James, in Madden's judgment, is that he had in fact advanced two forms of argument, one strong and one weak, and had subsequently vacillated between the two under different historical circumstances.[58] The stronger position, for which he was indebted to Charles Renouvier, holds that one has a duty as well as a right to believe,[59] whereas the later, weaker form of argument, for which he was indebted to Chauncey Wright, seems to permit belief under certain circumstances where evidence is inconclusive.

Kennedy also identifies two different doctrines – a 'right' to believe and a 'will' to believe – which he thinks have been 'sadly confused' by commentators.[60] Instead of distinguishing these chronologically, however, as Madden does, he finds them both contained, albeit not adequately delineated, in *The Will to Believe* itself. The *right* to believe is present when one is forced to make a momentous decision for which there is not adequate evidence. The *will* to believe has to do with what James calls self-verifying ideas – cases where 'faith creates its own verification.' Volition, on Kennedy's account, has a distinct and different role in each situation. In cases of self-verifying beliefs it can rightly play a prominent role in the formation of belief because the states of affairs involved in those cases contribute to the creation of the truth of the propositions involved. The formation of personal confidence, for example, that I can leap a wide mountain crevice is an important element in the eventual accomplishment of that feat. In cases of non-self-verifying beliefs, however, James denies to volition a comparable role.

The view that James had been misinterpreted was also held by F.C.S. Schiller. Schiller records that during a debate with Charles Strong, he had come to be convinced that the breadth of misunderstanding of James's *Will to Believe* was a function of the essay's demand for empirical verification being consistently ignored. For this reason, Schiller came to realize, James's appeal to will had been 'misconstrued ... as an incitement to make-believe, instead of as an analysis of the psychological process of acquiring beliefs.'[61] Schiller's interpretation of *The Will to Believe*, as later approved by James, was that 'a "will to find out" is an essential preliminary to finding out: in all knowing, it is the will which starts the process, while the final shape of our beliefs is moulded by the results of our experiments.'[62]

In sum, the dominant feature of the secondary literature on James's essay is the accusation that he advocated an unacceptable intrusion of the subject, as subject, into doxastic practice under certain special conditions, and that he confused belief and hypothesis-adoption. Dickinson Miller stands alone in having linked such concerns to the notion of liveness. Rejoinders by James's defenders have not responded in adequate depth and detail to what Miller clear-sightedly recognized was James's claim that the subject and world are related in the constitution of experience in such a way that probability and desirability are often very difficult, if not impossible, to disentangle introspectively in cases of live propositions. Why such a claim by James would not force him into an endorsement of wishful thinking has not been made adequately clear so far in the literature on *The Will to Believe*. My next step in trying to rectify such a situation will involve a closer scrutiny of what James has to say about liveness.

As I indicated in general terms in my opening comments of this book, what James was concerned about above all in *The Will to Believe* is the significance of *abandoning* or prohibiting the development of certain existing beliefs or propensities to believe, not in creating them. The longstanding neglect of this crucial feature of his position has been a function of a widespread disregard for one of the three main distinguishing characteristics of the options and propositions of interest to James in his essay: their liveness. It is to a recovery of the centrality of that aspect of James's essay that the remainder of this chapter is devoted.

At the outset of *The Will to Believe* James includes, alongside the forced and momentous nature of certain options or hypotheses of concern to his essay, the liveness of such options and hypotheses. Liveness possesses three main characteristics. The first of these has to do with belief. Liveness, says James in correspondence with Mark Baldwin concerning *The Will to Believe*, involves 'a will of complacence, assent, encouragement, towards *a belief already there*' (emphasis added),[63] and live theism in particular is described on a number of occasions in *The Will to Believe* in terms of religious 'belief,'[64] an 'active faith,'[65] and a 'believing attitude.'[66] James qualifies an identification of liveness with belief, however, by adding that the state he has in mind is 'not, of course, an absolute belief, but such beliefs as any of us have, strong inclinations to believe, but threatened.'[67] As he says regarding Pascal, 'unless there be some *pre-existing tendency to believe* in masses and holy water, the option offered to the will by Pascal is not a living option' (emphasis added).[68]

The main thesis statement of James's essay predicates such liveness of *options*, first and foremost, which are said to consist of competing live propositions whose evidential merits are as yet inconclusive. It would seem that liveness would not be a significant consideration in the choice between such propositions since both are themselves said to be live and neither is conclusively superior to the other evidentially. It has been generally assumed that in the absence of conclusive evidential considerations both alternatives make comparable claims on the subject and that the passional choice between them would be what James Wernham has called a 'pure gamble.' It is not difficult to understand how charges involving the intrusion of the subject and wishful thinking would follow closely upon the heels of such an understanding of James's position.

It is notable in this connection, however, that there is nothing in *The Will to Believe* which says that the competing live propositions in a live option are equally compelling or that there are no grounds whatever, apart from subjective preference, for the reasonableness of adopting one alternative over the other. As I will show below, there is a distinct imbalance, for example, between the alternatives in the case of the religious option, as it is portrayed by James. What is more, while evidential considerations are not sufficient to tip the balance decisively in one direction or the other in live options, it should be noted that James goes out of his way repeatedly to confine such evidential inconclusiveness to the level of 'pure reason,'[69] 'pure insight and logic,'[70] the 'purely judging mind,'[71] the 'pure intellect,'[72] and 'pure intellectualism.'[73] Moreover, when he defends theistic belief in particular, he stipulates that it is 'a defence of our right to adopt a believing attitude in religious matters, in spite of the fact that our *merely* logical intellect may not have been coerced' (emphasis added).[74] Such restrictions suggest that there are other considerations supportive of the reasonableness of sustaining a particular belief or propensity to believe, notwithstanding the appeals of its contrary, and I will later show why such influences play a significant role in James's case.

On the whole, then, with respect to the first major characteristic of liveness, I am proposing that James's main concern in *The Will to Believe* is with situations in which one has a certain existing belief or propensity to believe which, as he described it to Mark Baldwin, is 'threatened' by an alternative proposition towards which one also finds a propensity to believe. How ought one to proceed under such circumstances, James asks. I may, for example, find myself disposed to believe theistically but find as well that the gratuitous nature of suffering and evil in the world generates a propensity to believe otherwise. Am I entitled, James asks in *The Will to Believe* above all, to acquiesce in theism in spite of the propensity to believe its contrary, and in spite of insufficient empirical evidence to resolve the matter conclusively? What, in other words, would constitute intellectually responsible behaviour in relation to certain existing beliefs or propensities to believe? James's aim in *The Will to*

*Believe* is to defend the intellectual integrity of acquiescence in such beliefs.

That *The Will to Believe* argues along these lines emerges more clearly when James singles out the specifically religious option. Here, one encounters a distinctive but neglected level of James's case which has to do with a unique set of characteristics attributed by him to live theism. Live theism is deeply rooted in the 'heart' and the 'instincts,'[75] and 'good-will.'[76] It resides deep in one's nature, and it involves a tenacious 'passional need.'[77] It is far from being simply another intellectual possibility which may be casually adopted or dropped at will; it is, rather, '*forced on us we know not whence*' (emphasis added).[78] It is accompanied, moreover, by an uniquely persistent intuitive sense, among many people at least, that it must be met half-way if its evidential merits are to become fully apparent. It includes, that is, a peculiar sense that the pursuit of the truth in this domain involves a form of 'making willing advances,'[79] and engaging one's 'sympathetic nature,' in ways which may not be found in a purely abstract and detached analysis of theism. Live theism also often involves a distinctive noetic element, according to *The Varieties of Religious Experience*, and a distinctive experience of the world as well, for believers in the Western traditions of religion at least, for whom, in the light of such belief, 'the universe is no longer a mere *It* ... but a *Thou*.'[80] Live theism also generates an invigorating disposition, intellectual openness, and way of life to which James refers in 'The Moral Philosopher and the Moral Life' and *The Varieties of Religious Experience* as the 'strenuous mood.'

Nowhere in *The Will to Believe* or elsewhere in James's corpus does one find a depiction of the nontheistic alternatives in the religious option as possessing comparably formidable characteristics. The nontheistic alternatives in the live religious option may be 'threatening' in important respects, but are nowhere portrayed as having as deep a hold on human beings as theism.

The main question that James asks in *The Will to Believe*, concerns what constitutes responsible intellectual conduct in relation to live theism with this range of characteristics. I emphasize once again that James is concerned about a particular phenomenon, a widespread existing form of belief or propensity to believe. He is not advocating the manufacture of a new belief, much less the manufacture of a new belief for the self-serving purpose of deriving the exclusively personal benefits which may accrue from holding such a belief, and which will be shown later to be untenable. He asks, rather, what would constitute responsible intellectual conduct in relation to an existing theistic belief or propensity to believe which, while 'threatened,' nevertheless involves the foregoing host of distinctive characteristics.

However, there is more to liveness than its involvement with belief or a propensity to believe. Such belief builds upon an *intellectual* plausibility of a proposition for the subject, and here we encounter the second main characteristic of liveness. Such plausibility involves more than cultural familiarity, as might be suggested by James's example of the liveness to an Arab, by contrast with a non-Arab, of potential belief in the Mahdi. Nor is it a purely hypothetical possibility, as may be suggested by James's description of a live hypothesis as simply 'among the mind's options.' Anticipating the discomfort of his audience about the position he is developing, James warns near the end of *The Will to Believe* that those in attendance might well have been insufficiently attentive to the intellectual component of liveness:

> You ... are thinking, (perhaps without realizing it) of some particular religious hypothesis which for you is dead. The freedom to 'believe what we will' you apply to the case of some patent superstition; and the faith you think of is the faith defined by the schoolboy when he said 'Faith is when you believe something that you know ain't true.' I can only repeat that this is misapprehension. In concreto, the freedom to believe can only cover living options which the intellect of the individual cannot by itself resolve; and living options never seem absurdities to him who has them to consider.[81]

James contrasts a proposition which for a member of his audience is utterly implausible – a 'patent superstition' – with a proposition held by that audience member which, for that member at least, would be plausible ('living options never seem absurdities *to him* who has them to consider'). Who is qualified, James asks in a letter to Mark Baldwin about *The Will to Believe*, to make a judgment about such plausibility from without? What standard would allow for a determination of '*how* sincere' the conscientious individual is, or '*how* adequate or inadequate the "evidence" to him may seem?'[82] Numerous beliefs which are now widely vindicated seemed highly implausible to many people at the time of their emergence.

James's cautionary words regarding liveness near the end of *The Will to Believe* move in the same direction, drawing his audience's attention to the peculiar reasonableness of many propositions to those who hold them, notwithstanding the difficulty which such persons might experience in trying to articulate or defend such reasonableness. His audience, James suggests, ought not to envision *The Will to Believe* in terms of its indulgence of patently unjustifiable propositions held by someone else. Each individual in the audience, rather, ought to envision *The Will to Believe* in terms of its respect for the intellectual plausibility which certain propositions hold for responsible individuals to whom they so appear, notwithstanding the fact that such plausibility may be threatened in certain ways.

James calls for such respect in opposition to those in his audience and culture whose rejection of theism is the rejection of what they consider to be a 'patent superstition.' He is eager to challenge such dismissiveness as incompatible with the true temper of empiricism. The beliefs or propensities to believe of the kind with which he is concerned in his address, involving as they do the presence of a genuine, but threatened, intellectual plausibility to the subject, and the absence of evidential considerations which would decisively undermine such plausibility, may well turn out to be deserving of respectful benefit of the doubt. 'We ought ... delicately and profoundly to respect one another's mental freedom: then only shall we bring about the intellectual republic; then only shall we have that spirit of inner tolerance without which all our outer tolerance is soulless, and which is empiricism's glory; then only shall we live and let live in speculative as well as in practical things.'[83]

At this basic level, James's argument on behalf of intellectual openness could be invoked as readily for the purposes of defending atheism against an audience of smugly dogmatic theists, as it could be for a defence of theism under the circumstances in which James found himself. If the scales of plausibility in the religious option favour the nontheistic alternative for a particular conscientious individual, James would hold that acquiescence in the accompanying belief or propensity to believe nontheistically would receive support from the argument of *The Will to Believe*. Such support would not apply, however, to the fashionable anti-theism which James identified as the 'bogey' in response to which his essay was written, but would apply to a position which acknowledges the unnerving consequences of atheism, as these would later in the century be characterized by Sartre, for example, or to an agnosticism which is more than an atheism of convenience.

James's defence of intellectual tolerance and openness brings to the fore the third major characteristic of live propositions, and this has to do with the complex interdependence of many influences which give rise to liveness. This complexity makes the issue about what would constitute responsible behaviour towards live propositions a particularly difficult one, and raises questions about the simplistic character of recourse to evidence *per se* on the part of evidentialists such as Clifford.

In the century-long debate about *The Will to Believe*, as I indicated, only Dickinson Miller recognized not only the centrality of liveness to James's position, but the centrality to the notion of liveness of James's reticence about our ability in many cases to disentangle the respective contributions to liveness of numerous influences, personal and impersonal. Instead of exploring further why James would have held this position, Miller attacked it as necessarily leading to an intrusion of the subject in belief-formation. In so proceeding, Miller failed to explore some important elements of *The Will to Believe*, and other writings in James's corpus which support James's position.

With respect to *The Will to Believe* in particular, Miller failed to explore fully why James so strenuously develops his contention that in actual inquiry, 'pure insight and logic, whatever they might do ideally, are not the only things that really do produce our creeds.'[84] Most of *The Will to Believe* in fact labours to establish the complexity of the relationships among the many influences which 'really do produce our creeds,' and the essay does so, ultimately, with the purpose of thwarting the assuredness with which some members of James's audience and culture feel entitled to call for the abandonment of live propositions as complex and existentially influential as those involved in religious matters. The elusive way in which many influences intertwine in giving rise to the liveness of the propositions involved in such belief systems ought to raise serious questions about automatically impugning and overturning beliefs whose empirically evidential merits are as yet inconclusive. Norms of responsible intellectual conduct in relation to such live propositions must be developed with the complexity of liveness fully in view, James argues, lest, construing rationality too narrowly or simplistically, we adopt what will turn out in the long run to have been an 'irrational'[85] form of behaviour, a point to which I will return. The failure to take account of all such influences in the development of norms for responsible intellectual conduct risks creating only a facade of doxastic responsibility behind which subjectivity may continue to exercise a powerful and unregulated influence, as James argues that it does even in Clifford's case.

On the face of it, Clifford seems to have provided a sensible response to the complexity of the intellectual life. In cases which preclude a disentangling of the many foregoing influences, we ought to waive our assent until we become able to decide matters more clearly, and thereby protect a firm evidential basis for the life of belief. One of James's main aims in *The Will to Believe* is to put such a position to the test in light of the complexity of the life of reason which he labours at length to illustrate. Does such counsel from Clifford embody the elimination of the potentially distorting influence of subjectivity in belief formation, or does it in the end only offer an alternative form of involvement for passional nature in belief-formation?

Unfortunately, James argues, Clifford's evidentialism only offers an alternative form of involvement for passional nature in belief-formation. In his preoccupation with avoiding error, James observes, Clifford is rightly 'critical of many of his desires and fears.'[86] Nevertheless, his 'fear [of error] he slavishly obeys,' and to this fear his evidentialism is heavily indebted. The depth of this indebtedness is of great interest to James in *The Will to Believe*, given the widespread fashionability of positions like Clifford's. It is striking that decades of vigorous criticism of James for having condoned the intrusion of sentiment in doxastic practice have not been accompanied by a comparably vigorous pursuit of the significance of James's charge that this intrusion lies at the heart of Clifford's own evidentialism. Even Clifford has not been able to disentangle the many influences at work in his own evidentialism.

I will return to other aspects of James's critique of Clifford. For now, I wish only to point out that even James's analysis of Clifford has the complexity of liveness as its backdrop. The degree to which James's emphasis on the intertwining of influences in liveness has been neglected in scholarship is surprising. What one finds in the work of most commentators is a routine compartmentalization of such influences which does not take notice of, much less engage or overturn, James's pivotal contention that in the case of many live propositions such influences *together* constitute liveness in a way which is often complicated enough to preclude such compartmentalization.[87] Even a cursory overview of the structure of *The Will to Believe* reveals that James is far more interested in pursuing this matter than he is in anything else. His engagement of it takes the form of a long digression which actually makes up the bulk of *The Will to Believe*. Note, for example, that in a work consisting of ten sections, the section as near to the end as Part VIII begins by saying 'now, *after all this introduction*, let us go straight at our question' (emphasis added).[88] Only near the end of the essay, does James get around to dealing with the forced and momentous character of the options which he had announced at the outset as the special concern of his address.

The delay is clearly intentional. He says in Part IV, for instance, after having already presented a good deal of material, that he is going to do even more 'preliminary work.' He promises in Part VII that his 'preliminaries' will soon be done. In fact, between the end of Part I and the middle of Part VIII the forced and momentous character of certain options is referred to only once, and this in a summary one-sentence thesis statement in Part IV.[89] It is a parenthetical exploration of 'the actual psychology of human opinion,'[90] and an exploration of the relations among the many influences which 'really do produce our creeds,' which extends all the way from the end of Part I, in which James defines forced and momentous options, to Part VIII where he returns to that subject.

When we try to inventory the influences which really do produce our creeds, James points out in this long digression, we encounter an enormously complex intellectual scene. At first, he concedes, it appears as though with most of our convictions we 'could do nothing when the intellect had once said its say.'[91] It certainly seems, for example, that the conviction that I am in physical pain or that Abraham Lincoln existed or that two one-dollar bills do not add up to one hundred dollars, are independent of any volitional influence. 'The talk of believing by our volition seems, then, from one point of view, simply silly.'[92] From the point of view of the sciences, moreover, the notion that the subject is to play a significant role in the development of human conviction 'is worse than silly, it is "vile."'[93] The cornerstone of the scientific ideal is disinterestedness, 'patience,' 'postponement,' 'choking down of preference,' as Huxley and Clifford would have it.[94] Moreover, James concedes willingly, 'all this strikes one as healthy ... Free will and simply wishing do seem, in the matter of our credences, to be only fifth wheels to the coach.'[95]

Closer scrutiny, however, reveals that a great many convictions, especially those involved in religious, ethical and political belief systems, for example, are deeply indebted to the influence of 'fear and hope, prejudice and passion, imitation and partisanship, and circumpressure of our caste and set' as well as influences 'born of the intellectual climate.'[96] Among the listeners in James's audience, he notes for instance, there are many who have strong convictions about the democratic system or about molecular physics. Their convictions are rooted not just in knowledge of political science or physics but in social consensus as well – 'the intellectual climate.' The personal willingness on the part of people to embrace certain prestigious conventions in these intellectual domains plays a formidable role in their beliefs. Moreover, the commonplace unwillingness to even consider certain propositions whose unfashionability disposes one to reject them out of hand is in many cases rooted not in any serious analysis of the intellectual merits of the positions involved, but in personal and societal 'passional tendencies and volitions [which] run *before* ... [by contrast with others which run] after belief.' Those which run before, of which we are scarcely even aware much of the time, are major influences in the ability to recognize the potential or actual intellectual merits of those propositions.

There are, in other words, many different influences which give rise to the liveness – and deadness – of particular propositions. James was particularly concerned about this phenomenon in the case of theism whose cultural fortunes, as I have indicated, he believed, were on the decline, and it was the spectre of this decline, which motivated James to write *The Will to Believe*.

However, all this is only the beginning of the story. Even the adoption of basic systems of thought – scientific, geometric, moral, religious, aesthetic, mathematical and so on – is a complex activity which requires extensive involvement by the subject. There is no unambiguous evidential basis for the conviction that scientific categories are productive of completely trustworthy truths. The same holds for the conviction that there is such a thing as truth.[97] So too, 'moral scepticism can no more be refuted or proved by logic than intellectual scepticism can.'[98] In ethics, 'the question of having moral beliefs at all or not having them is decided by our will.'[99] In axiology, the same applies: 'to compare the *worths*, both of what exists and of what does not exist, we must consult not science, but what Pascal calls our heart.'[100] Moreover:

> Science herself consults her heart when she lays it down that the infinite ascertainment of fact and correction of false belief are the supreme goods for man. Challenge the statement, and science can

only repeat it oracularly, or else prove it by showing that such ascertainment and correction bring man all sorts of other goods which man's heart in turn declares.[101]

The same applies in many cases even to evidence itself: 'one's conviction that the evidence one goes by is of the real objective brand, is only one more subjective opinion added to the lot. For what a contradictory array of opinions have objective evidence and absolute certitude been claimed!'[102]

A comparable involvement of the subject in the life of reason can be observed in the way in which actual scientists and researchers go about their work. This is something for which the principles of empiricism make allowance by looking to the consequences rather than to the origins of belief, for it is often not possible to segregate the exact role of the subject in the origin and maintenance of a particular line of inquiry. Actual practice in the process of inquiry involves personal dispositions towards intellectual possibilities which evidentially do not yet warrant such dispositions. The actual scientific researcher in the concrete situation is often 'in love with some pet "live hypothesis" of his own;'[103] the chemist sufficiently 'taken' with a particular hypothesis in many instances that he is willing to act, to spend time exploring its viability.[104]

James nowhere denies that the world independent of the subject exerts a significant influence upon the formation of many convictions. As I will show in the next chapter, there is a pronounced and widely neglected realist vein in his epistemology. What he argues is that it is often not possible to isolate such extra-subjective influences entirely from other influences involving the subject and the community in a way which would satisfy Clifford's invocation of evidence *per se*. It is often not possible, that is, to isolate 'intellectual insight,' – *'pure* reason' – from 'wish and will' in the development of belief. 'If any one should ... assume that intellectual insight is what remains after wish and will and sentimental preference have taken wing, or that pure reason is what then settles our opinions, he would fly quite as directly in the teeth of the facts.'[105] It is only with a view to such facts that realistic norms of responsible conduct in relation to certain existing beliefs or propensities to believe can be developed. The more closely one examines such facts, the more one is compelled to ask whether, notwithstanding the widely shared contention that 'objective evidence and certitude are doubtless very fine ideals to play with ... where on this moonlit and dream-visited planet are they found?'[106] While the 'dispassionately judicial intellect ... ought to be our ideal,' James willingly concedes, it remains the case that the processes by which actual human beings concretely live out an intellectual relationship with the world at many levels make the establishment of conclusive evidential credentials for beliefs concerning complex matters very difficult.

Vivid testimony to this difficulty can be found in the exceedingly long history of manifest diversity and fallibility in philosophical inquiry, observes James, notwithstanding perennial appeals to evidence and sound argument. One finds evidentially and argumentatively developed cases both for and against the reasonableness of the world; the existence of a personal deity or of an extra-mental domain; the possibility of foundations for moral principles; the possibility of the world being eternal, of will being free, or the universe being finite, as well as many political and moral positions, and even scientific ones as well. Apart from relations of ideas, one can in fact 'find no proposition ever regarded by any one as evidently certain that has not either been called a falsehood, or at least had its truth sincerely questioned by some one else,'[107] invocations of evidence notwithstanding.

Not only has inquiry generated conflicts of the foregoing sorts throughout history, so too has the quest for criteria to adjudicate such conflicts. Appeal to consensus, intuition, instinct, perception, logic, evidence, common sense, revelation, and many others have all been seriously proposed and found wanting. In the end, 'no concrete test of what is really true has ever been agreed upon.'[108] The history of human inquiry amply illustrates that the 'intellect, even with truth directly in its grasp, may have no infallible signal for knowing whether it be truth or no,'[109] and 'in a world where we are so certain to incur ... [errors] in spite of all our caution, a certain lightness of heart seems healthier than ... [Clifford's] excessive nervousness on their behalf.'[110]

Commentators have not only failed to do justice to the centrality, in *The Will to Believe*, of James's efforts to establish the complexity of the influences which *together* give rise to liveness, but they have also failed to recognize the congruence between this aspect of his essay and work elsewhere in his corpus where he greatly broadens his account of such complexity. Before exploring the details of this congruence, however, a brief comment is needed to justify such a contextualization, for in 1907 James wrote to Horace Kallen that *The Will to Believe* should be kept distinct from his other work.[111]

There are two sets of considerations which ought to prevent this passing comment by James from prohibiting a contextualization of *The Will to Believe*. First, as Ralph Barton Perry pointed out, the letter in which James makes such a recommendation

> while it divides the doctrine of 'pragmatism' and the 'will to believe,' also points the way to their union. For if verification is a sort of 'satisfactoriness' then truth becomes in some broad sense commensurable with those subjective values which justify belief in the absence of verification. So the way is paved for the general idea of truth as the goodness of ideas on the whole, where agreement with fact, though it may take precedence, is only one value among others.[112]

John Wild, as well, has shown that 'these statements [encouraging a separation of *The Will to Believe*] were made for special purposes, and cannot be taken too seriously. They have a biographic rather than a systematic significance.'[113] James Wernham upholds the separation that James recommended, but his argument on behalf of this position depends on his own distinctive contention, in relation to *The Will to Believe*, that 'we have no intellectual ground for believing ... [theism],'[114] and so must make a 'pure gamble' – a position which I will show to be untenable.

The second consideration which ought to prevent James's comment from prohibiting a contextualization of *The Will to*

*Believe* is the degree to which that essay itself borrows liberally from James's thought on many subjects including volition, belief, and so on, thought which seems on the whole to have remained generally stable over many years in important respects. Such stability is not a surprising phenomenon, given the relatively late stage in his career at which he began producing his major works, and the resulting shortness of time which elapsed between the publication of the *Principles,* and his later writings about religion and about Radical Empiricism. While some sections of the *Principles* were developed during his earlier career, that work as a whole was completed and published only when James was 49 years of age. While it is 'early' in terms of the sequence of his literary output, it is not early in terms of his life or of the development of his thought.

A demonstration on my part of the general coherence in James's work would needlessly duplicate what has already been done widely and thoroughly. It is true that James made significant changes in his position on the relation of knower and object known, for example, and I will note these in due course. Such change as did occur after the production of the *Principles,* however, is often foreshadowed even in that early work. The dualism of knower and known, for instance, which is admittedly more prominent in earlier writing, can already be seen breaking down within the *Principles* itself. One can trace here 'the demise of dualism in the *Principles,*' as Wilshire, Edie, and others, have shown, 'and the emergence of phenomenal monism and incipient phenomenology.'[115] The extensive work of both Charlene Seigfried and Gerald Myers, among others, also supports the judgment that substantial continuity exists between James's early and later work on this subject. Both authors underscore the provisionality of the methodological priorities which lay behind James's dualism of knower and known in the *Principles*. The purpose of the *Principles* had been to further the development of psychology as a natural science. James worked hard, therefore, at restraining his spontaneous philosophical impulse, given the relevant methodological restraints involved in psychology conceived of as a natural science, to engage in what he even early on saw as the philosophical need to question dualism. Notwithstanding the periodically dualistic language in the *Principles*, then, there are signs in that work itself of the more unified view of Radical Empiricism which, as John J. McDermott once put it, 'was simmering but had not yet been announced.'

The high level of detail in Myers' outstanding study of James has contributed a good deal to illuminating continuity among the various stages and parts of James's thought on many other issues as well. These include his contention that perceptual experience of the world is pervasively informed by human interest. Such a position long predates even the *Principles*, Myers shows, and endures throughout James's career. James always denied that

> knowledge is ever simply impressed upon one who only passively feels things. The active participation of the knower is required in noticing, attending, naming, classifying, and predicting; without it there would be only feeling and acquaintance but no genuine knowledge. Active attending or noticing is equated with willing, which led Perry to say that the most important of James's insights in psychology was that knowledge depends ultimately upon will. This idea, customarily associated with his later writings on pragmatism and religion, was already consolidated in *Principles*.[116]

Edie has made similar observations.[117]

James's later view that mental states can be compounded of other mental states, Myers also shows, originated as early as 1895 in the essay, 'The Knowing of Things Together,' a piece written a year before *The Will to Believe*.[118] Moreover, James's concerns, in line with Bergson's, about the distorting effect that conceptualization can have on the flow of immediate experience may have been held even while he was writing the *Principles*.[119] In addition, the links between will, attention, intellectual life and psychological health also date back to the *Principles*.[120] So too do James's accounts of the nature of thought found in 'Philosophical Conceptions and Practical Results,' the inaugural essay on Pragmatism.[121] As for the distinction between subjectivity and objectivity, while James's thought attains greater maturity in his later philosophy of Radical Empiricism, the signs of that maturity can be found in early writings.[122] Equally traceable to such earlier thought are his positions on self and on free will.[123]

Even Pragmatism itself, Myers has illustrated, 'was first formulated in *Principles*.'[124] For its part, Radical Empiricism as well can be found already emerging in the 1885 essay, 'The Function of Cognition,' and in the 1895 essay, 'The Knowing of Things Together,' writings which Perry left out of the 1912 collection of *Essays in Radical Empiricism*. The particular doctrine of Radical Empiricism that mind and its objects are two aspects of pure experience, while maturing relatively late in James's career, nevertheless rested upon an insight which 'had been attractive to him even some years prior to the completion of *Principles*, and it was responsible for the doubts about Cartesian dualism sprinkled throughout that book.'[125]

It was one of John Wild's particular achievements to have illustrated the extent to which Radical Empiricism 'presupposes the whole of his earlier Psychology to be properly understood.'[126] James Edie has shown likewise that the *Principles* 'lays the groundwork for all his later more popular essays and lectures.'[127] John J. McDermott's analyses as well have established that 'the "psychology," "will to believe," "radical empiricism," and "pragmatism" are of a piece in his [James's] philosophy.'[128] Kauber and Hare have argued even more radically that the only way of making *The Will to Believe* intelligible is by setting it in the context of James's philosophy as a whole.[129] They contend not only that James's larger philosophy assists one in interpreting *The Will to Believe*, but that on particular issues 'the remainder of James's philosophy virtually dictates' a certain interpretation of the essay.[130] Among Edie, Wild, McDermott, Seigfried, Myers, and others, then, can be found significant agreement to the effect that James's later work tends on many major subjects to articulate with greater maturity, rather than to overturn entirely, 'lines already laid down'[131] in the *Principles*.

Given these considerations, I will contextualize *The Will to Believe* when the essay appears to be significantly indebted to aspects of James's thought developed outside of it. This will be the case particularly with respect to James's account of the complex unity of immediate experience, for it is only within such terms of reference that the role assigned by James to passional nature in connection with liveness and the strenuous mood can be grasped as James intended.

What *The Will to Believe* has to say about liveness and the complexity of the intellectual life is only an abbreviated form of a position developed much more extensively throughout James's writings. He inquires at great length and with considerable insight in a number of his works into the labyrinthine character of the intellectual life, and these inquiries have direct application to an appreciation of liveness and, as I will show, to the ways in which the role of passional nature in *The Will to Believe* stands within the context of the complex unity of immediate experience which circumscribes its influence.

Regarding this complex unity, even individual terms much less complex beliefs, do not stand alone but are suffused with the many nuances of meaning which they derive from the public language in which they stand, and the particular propositions in which they occur. Such propositions are themselves no less indebted to yet wider contexts involving an interdependence with other propositions whose influence they bear as 'fringes,'[132] 'haloes,'[133] and 'suffusions.'[134] As James puts it on one occasion, 'the present image shoots its perspective far before it'[135] in such a way that acts of understanding rarely if ever possess a clearly definable conceptual limit, but involve a host of 'unarticulated affinities'[136] among the elements which constitute them.

While one may say, then, that the '*intrinsically* important'[137] elements of discourse are the grammatically substantive ones, the 'halting places' constituted by subjects and predicates, this formulation misses the 'delicate idiosyncrasy'[138] of the intellectual life. That idiosyncrasy is a function of the complexity with which many relations together contribute to forming the full meaning of each assertion, 'with every word fringed and the whole sentence bathed in that original halo of obscure relation, which, like a horizon, then spreads about its meaning.'[139]

The meaning of particular propositions is deeply implicated in such constellations of relations. 'The same object is known everywhere, now from the point of view, if we may so call it, of this word, now from the point of view of that. And in our feeling of each word there chimes an echo or foretaste of every other.'[140] One can envision a term as lying at the intersection of a variety of trajectories of meaning, like a mathematical point at the intersection of many lines. It can 'appear' differently depending on the perspective.[141] 'The object of every thought,' then, 'is neither more nor less than *all* that the thought thinks, exactly as the thought thinks it, however complicated the matter' (emphasis added).[142]

'However complicated the matter' is the main point here, returning to a central theme in my study. Propositions are not isolated; their meaning and plausibility are a *contextual* phenomenon. They possess their liveness or deadness by virtue of occupying a particular location within a vast field of awareness which includes many interrelations, and such a 'field' view of awareness plays a major part in James's account of the sorts of insights which *The Varieties of Religious Experience* illustrates as underwriting much theistic belief.[143] Meaning and plausibility are highly context-dependent, a position richly articulated more recently in connection with theism by Iris Murdoch.[144]

An appreciation of contextualization must also take into consideration the impact of volitional, social and historical influences as well, James rightly adds. As an individual, for example, I am able to choose to view my relations to elderly and demanding parents in light of their life-long efforts and sacrifices on my behalf, or in light of their faults and failures. How I *see* my moral obligations towards them, and how I act, will be deeply affected by such choices. These deliberations, moreover, are inseparable from the vast webs of convictions and sentiments involved in, for example, a Japanese or American cultural context, and the history of such contexts, within which deliberation transpires. Behind James's assertion in *The Will to Believe* that all thought is 'funded' lies his recognition of this feature of intellectual life, a recognition that in a great many matters, '*our fundamental ways of thinking about things are discoveries of exceedingly remote an-*

*cestors, which have been able to preserve themselves throughout the experience of all subsequent time.* They form one great stage of equilibrium in the human mind's development, the stage of *common sense.*'[145]

Such bodies of belief are assimilated by succeeding generations and become entrenched over time to the point of forming the bedrock of much that constitutes conventional thought. Conventional beliefs are 'the dead heart of the living tree' with their own 'palaeontology;' they constitute a core 'grown stiff with years of veteran service and petrified in men's regard by sheer antiquity.'[146] This petrification takes the form of some such beliefs seeming to be virtually self-evident, an impression so strong that in the case of some common conceptions, 'we are now incapable of thinking naturally in any other terms.'[147] It is important to note the connection between this point and James's suggestion in *The Will to Believe* that even in the case of some beliefs which *appear* to involve nothing but intellectual influences, there may nevertheless be other influences very much at work.

It is not just complexity which James is at pains to exhibit as characteristic of the intellectual field, however, but also a unity which permeates this complexity. Here, a distinctive coherentist element of his epistemology emerges. The indebtedness of the intellectual life to unity is revealed in a number of ways, not the least of which is the difficulty of introducing into current thought, contentions whose novelty threatens unity. The introduction of radium into the conventional understanding of physics in the early twentieth century, for example, constituted a profound challenge to the status quo of that discipline,[148] as did the introduction of Descartes's geometric analyses in relation to those of Euclid.[149] These became live only slowly, as ongoing deliberation on them clarified their relation to the intellectual *status quo*. Such new proposals had to acquit themselves successfully in relation to the overall coherence of existing thought, upon which thought depends heavily for its intelligibility.

We must *talk* consistently just as we must *think* consistently: for both in talk and thought we deal with kinds. Names are arbitrary, but once understood they must be kept to. We must not now call Abel 'Cain' or Cain 'Abel.' If we do, we ungear ourselves from the whole book of Genesis, and from all its connections with the universe of speech and fact down to the present time. We throw ourselves out of whatever truth that entire system of speech and fact may embody.[150]

Such coherence, James suggests, can be likened to the key in which music is composed, a key which runs through all the variations in a particular composition, or likened to the original architectural plan of a building which endures through additions and alterations of the structure: 'you can make great changes but you cannot change a Gothic Church into a Doric temple.'[151] This balance is not something which the subject is at liberty simply to ignore in the interests of personal benefit, for 'the greatest enemy of any one of our truths may be the rest of our truths.'[152]

Whether in *The Will to Believe*, the *Principles*, *Pragmatism*, *Radical Empiricism*, or elsewhere in James's corpus, he returns repeatedly to the theme of the complex unity of the interrelation of many influences in the intellectual life, and to this can also be added a number of additional considerations involved in his extensive attack on associationism. Physiological influences, for example, play a crucial role in the varying capacities among people to discriminate, abstract, generalize, and to generate concepts, as distinct from simply utilizing already existing ones.[153] The mere repetitive presence of objects even to neurophysiologically developed knowers does not by itself account fully for the initial acquisition of the concepts of those objects. *'The manner in which we now become acquainted with complex objects need not in the least resemble the manner in which the original elements of our consciousness grew up.'*[154]

The ability to form a concept of an unfamiliar kind of animal, for instance, is a complex event in which a good many historical encounters with other animals, biting things, pets, and so on are simultaneously at work. Given this history, I am as an adult 'already in possession of categories for knowing each and all of its several attributes, and of a memory for retracing the order of their conjunction.'[155] The original acquisition of these categories, however, is not so easily accounted for by such encounters with the world. Their original acquisition seems, rather, to involve in a central way fortuitous neurological developments which happily, although without our being able to fathom exactly how, have allowed for intellectual purchase on the world. Religious concepts are implicated here as deeply as are biological, mathematical, or other ones.

One must also take account of 'secondary internal processes, which vary enormously from brain to brain, even though the brains be exposed to exactly the same "outer relations."'[156] Such 'indirect causes of mental modifications,' while not fully understood, are nonetheless reflected clearly in a wide variety of intellectual aptitudes.[157] One person, for example, may have a profound appreciation of music and another not; one may take to being at sea and another not; one may be gifted in the visual arts and another not.[158] The same applies to the distinctive aptitudes of individuals for humour, for poetry, or for mathematics, none of which abilities are unambiguously traceable to their possessors' direct experience of the world.[159]

The same influences can be felt in the area of ethics as well. While commending Mill for underscoring the indebtedness of many moral convictions to their association with pleasure, for example, James also points out that 'it is surely impossible to explain all our [ethical] sentiments and preferences in this simple way.'[160] Association between the imputation of goodness and the presence of pleasure or utility fails to account for many 'secondary affections' which originate independently of such association. Some individuals – Dag Hammarskjöld in his work as Secretary General of the United Nations, for example – have possessed a particular aptitude for forming complex and profound moral judgments, while other individuals, such as the pacifist Tolstoy, have exhibited a novelty of moral insight which is not usually found among their contemporaries with whom they share a common disposition to the pleasurable.[161] *The Varieties of Religious Experience* presents copious evidence that there exist among many individuals analogous aptitudes having to do with religion. The conceptual results of such 'inner forces' –

'brain-born' neurological propensities, James calls them – 'supervene upon experience' in such a way that they alter the character of other experiences of the world, however direct and concrete.

Permeating the intellectual field is also the influence of certain personal initiatives which are indispensable in the successful undertaking of any intellectual inquiry, as James argued in *The Will to Believe*. Basic scientific contentions concerning, for example, the uniformity of nature must be held 'in spite of the most rebellious appearances; and our conviction of its truth is far more like a religious faith than like assent to a demonstration.'[162] While one part of the body of experience as a whole supports the belief that there is consistency in the natural order – the infant learns to anticipate being fed when the nurse appears but not when the sibling appears – there also grows a contrary body of experience as well. 'The order of scientific thought is quite incongruent either with the way in which reality exists or with the way in which it comes before us.'[163] In many instances, events simply do not develop as anticipated. As Sigwart put it in his *Logic*, James points out in *Principles*:

> Whereas a part of these associations grows confirmed by frequent repetition, another part is destroyed by contradictory experiences; and the world becomes divided for us into two provinces, one in which we are at home and anticipate with confidence always the same sequences; another filled with alternating, variable, accidental occurrences.[164]

So ambiguous is actual experience when taken in its entirety that it precludes any wholly empirical justification of belief in the uniformity of nature. 'From the point of view of strict empiricism, nothing exists but the sum of particular perceptions with their coincidences on the one hand, their contradictions on the other.'[165] Concrete experience gives direct access only to truths regarding 'the proximate laws of nature, and habitudes of concrete things, that heat melts ice, that salt preserves meat, that fish die out of water, and the like.'[166] Any inference from such limited convictions to an overarching assertion of the complete uniformity of nature as a whole cannot be defended empirically. It depends, on the contrary, on the personal choice to disregard significant segments of experience.

Taking the foregoing considerations into account, the results of scientific investigation can be called the direct 'result of experience' only in a remote sense; they are 'no more ... inward *reproductions* of the outer order than the ethical and aesthetic relations are.'[167] Rather, 'the most persistent relations which science believes in are never matters of experience at all, but have to be disengaged from under experience by a process of elimination, that is, by ignoring conditions which are always present.'[168] The compelling nature of scientific understanding is a function in significant part, it turns out, not only of a dispositional willingness to accept certain points of departure but also of the '*inward* thought-necessity' which belongs to the *a priori* ideal system of scientific concepts being brought to the world and applied selectively to it. Thus 'the popular notion that "Science" is forced on the mind *ab extra*, and that our interests have nothing to do with its constructions, is utterly absurd.'[169] The *intermixture* of such interests and the influence of the world generates a scientific process which is actually remarkably roundabout. The scientific *status quo* at any one time represents the distillation of relatively few convictions from a large number of others which have proven inadequate and so have been discarded.[170] 'For one [scientific conception] that proves useful and applicable there are a thousand that perish through their worthlessness.'[171]

The process of generating scientific hypotheses introduces a further element into the complexity of the life of reason, and the liveness of certain conceptions. The emergence of hypotheses, James points out, is very often 'akin to that of the flashes of poetry and sallies of wit to which the instable brain-paths equally give rise.'[172] Dickinson Miller was seen to take great exception to James's assigning of importance to such a peculiar flash of insight, an *aperçu* which resists adjudication by conventional methods of empirical inquiry.

In the cases of Newton and Darwin, however, James observes, this seems to be precisely the sort of intellectual activity upon which much of the rest of their more mundane work was ultimately dependent. 'The flash of similarity between an apple and the moon, between the rivalry for food in nature and the rivalry for man's selection, was too recondite to have occurred to any but exceptional minds,'[173] and the peculiar ability to *see* such novel relations is a fundamental, albeit poorly understood element of rational behaviour.

How different the human being is from other animals in this respect, James recognized. Contrary to the stereotype that James's appeals to utility in epistemology led him to subordinate the intellectual life to what is familiar and personally desirable, what he in fact realized is that it is non-human animals whose experience is dominated by obvious relations. They are able quickly to learn, for example, to behave differently at the smell of a skunk or that of fresh fruit, but they are also dominated by such predictable associations. Human beings, however, while exhibiting such behaviour, which James calls association 'by contiguity' in order to designate the obvious nature of the associations recognized, are strikingly different in being able to identify relations in the midst of an apparent total lack of relation, and to build systems of understanding and belief on such insights.[174]

The metaphorical ability to juxtapose apparently unrelated entities in such a way as to bring forth previously unrecognized relations among them is central to scientific, artistic, religious, poetic, and all other forms of thought. The centrality of metaphor does not diminish the importance of methodologically regulated forms of inquiry such as those of logical and scientific analysis, however, and James does not try to force a standoff on this count in *The Will to Believe* or elsewhere, in spite of his essay's periodic rhetorical criticisms of science and logic. Science, instead, is relocated by James among, rather than above, a wide range of intellectual activities, all of which are shown to capitalize in different ways on the root human metaphorical capacity.

In other words, James 'dislodges scientific explanations as paradigmatic for all explanations by showing that such explanation itself is a subset of the creative imposition of form.'[175] Overall, then, 'the ability to recognize unusual couplings, to discern relationships where no one has yet seen them, is the basis for both scientific and poetic genius.'[176] It is also, Seigfried neglects to say, a central element of religious thought, as James points out in *The Varieties of Religious Experience*. Rule-governed procedures of thought rely and build upon this more basic capacity for insight, and the capacity to relate experienced entities creatively in keeping with such insight.

Few analysts have appreciated better than Charlene Seigfried James's redefinition of rationality in terms of the human metaphorical capacity. It is essential to James's epistemology that it looks to such metaphorical capacities in its effort to 'combine the notion of careful and exact observation, which is characteristic of the natural sciences, with observation as romantic vision, the act of "seeing into" as practised by Emerson, Tennyson, Whitman and his other favourite poets;'[177] to integrate 'seeing as exactness, seeing as worthiness, and seeing as "feeling with."'[178]

> James's practice of sympathetic concrete observation brings together as a unified process 'seeing' and 'seeing into,' that is, seeing as scientific observation whose ideal is exactness and seeing as poetic transfiguration whose ideal is worthiness. The rare ability 'to seize fresh aspects in concrete things' is inextricably perceptive and inventive at the same time and characterizes the great scientist as well as the great artist.[179]

It is a pity that Seigfried's outstanding analysis of James in this respect is never brought to bear in detail upon his account of religiosity, for live theism, as James shows in *The Varieties of Religious Experience*, is rooted in great part in peculiar insights of a certain kind about which more will be said later.

Further aspects of the third characteristic of liveness – the complex unity of the influences which together give rise to it – could be added to those so far set out, but that complexity is sufficiently clear by now, I hope. The liveness or deadness of particular propositions or belief systems has to do with an extraordinarily complex field of relations which involves extensive interdependence among its many elements. Particular beliefs, much less large belief systems which are as complex as those involved in religion, ethics and politics, implicate an incalculable number of intertwining historical, cultural, linguistic, temperamental, neurological, volitional, and other influences. Even the brief foregoing digression into this matter reveals a scene so complex that the prospect of trying introspectively to disentangle these many threads in the pursuit of conclusive evidence in matters as complex as theism is at the very least extremely daunting, if not destined from the outset to failure.

These considerations should be kept prominently in mind in connection with James's contention in *The Will to Believe*, that the state of things in the intellectual life is 'far from simple;'[180] it is in fact very mixed up. Therefore, he concludes, 'our next duty, having recognized this mixed-up state of affairs, is to ask whether it be simply reprehensible and pathological, or whether, on the contrary, we must treat it as a normal element in making up our minds.'[181] As it turns out, the complex interplay of many diverse influences is in fact a normal element in the conduct of the life of reason. It is an element, however, which greatly complicates the nature of liveness, and the development of realistic norms of intellectually responsible behaviour towards live propositions. James's concern is to maintain such complexity clearly in view when developing norms of responsible intellectual behaviour in relation to certain existing beliefs or propensities to believe which, while they cannot be decisively vindicated evidentially at the moment, nevertheless possess a genuine, albeit threatened, intellectual plausibility for the subject.

It is important once again to emphasize that in *The Will to Believe* it is certain existing beliefs or propensities to believe which concern James, and he asks difficult and long-neglected questions about purportedly evidentialist calls, such as those of Clifford, for what would amount to an abandonment of these beliefs. Can we conclusively show, while keeping in mind the foregoing complexity of the intellectual life, that abandonment necessarily serves the pursuit of truth as well as the avoidance of error? For that matter, does it even serve the avoidance of error, in the end? The complexity of the relationships among the influences which give rise to liveness makes the pursuit of objectivity in belief something much more complex than sweeping appeals to evidence *per se*, as I will show in the next chapter.

# 3

# Subjectivity and Belief

One of the most widespread and serious charges against James's philosophy of religion throughout this century has been the charge that it endorses wishful thinking. Accusations in this vein have been evoked above all by James's advocacy of the involvement of passional nature in the life of belief, by his claim, that is, that a significant role in shaping belief ought to be given to 'our subjective nature, feelings, emotions, and propensities.'[1] It has been generally assumed that in the absence of clear evidential considerations, subjective states would enjoy a degree of autonomy in their influence on belief which is conducive to wishful thinking, an influence which such states would not have if, as Clifford suggests, greater restraint were exercised in anticipation of better evidence.

I will argue in this chapter that within the terms of reference of James's account of the intellectual life, as contextually complex as I have shown that to be, subjective influences do not enjoy the degree of autonomy imputed to them by James's critics, and that the longstanding charges of wishful thinking should be reassessed with a view to this fact. It is a great many commentators, not James, who have compartmentalized the life of reason in a way which isolates the many influences actually involved in it from one another, and it is those commentators, therefore, not James, who have laid the groundwork for the isolation of subjective influences which has led to charges of wishful thinking. For his part, James depicted subjective states as framed and limited in their influence in the long run by their interrelations within the complex unity of immediate experience, and by their interrelations with the many different kinds of consequences which flow from particular beliefs.

Not all commentators have been equally remiss in neglecting the contextual setting of James's recourse to passional nature. Gerald Myers, for example, has been an exception in this respect, recognizing that, for James, subjective influences do not stand alone; they 'exist as they do because something in reality harmonizes with them.'[2] Notwithstanding his recognition of this aspect of James's position, however, even Myers eventually goes on to sever such states from the larger setting which he has indicated is provided for them by James, and proceeds to criticize James for sponsoring wishful thinking.

John J. McDermott stands apart in having recognized not only that there is a restrictive context in which subjective states exert their influence, but also that James's assignment of epistemological significance to these states is limited in important ways by that context. While recognizing, with Myers and others, that 'the active relationship between "congeniality" as a character of the real, and the "powers" of men, is a central insight in the thought of James,' McDermott rightly adds that:

> although he [James] sees truth as a function of 'interest,' this position does not encourage predatory action, for the dialectic between man's 'powers' and the 'congeniality' of nature is always framed out within the demanding context of empirically given relationships. Further, this interaction leads James ... constantly to set all human activity into the wider process of 'seeing and feeling the total push and pressure of the cosmos.'[3]

Only when this aspect of James's thought is clarified do the weaknesses of the longstanding charges of wishful thinking make themselves apparent.

James is known for his efforts to integrate human purpose, intention, and sentiment into epistemology.[4] Many philosophers recoil from what they see as the result of James's efforts in this respect: 'a universe with such as *us* contributing to create its truth, a world delivered to *our* opportunism and *our* private judgments.'[5] Such a world seems to them to be 'a trunk without a tag, a dog without a collar,'[6] an open-ended event which is not so much for humans to replicate reliably in an intellectual mirror, as it is something to interpret in ways which seem uncomfortably susceptible to self-service. The prominence of this aspect of James's work has often evoked the sorts of negative response which more recently can be found among some critics of Richard Rorty.

Rorty and others have contributed a good deal to a wider recognition of the involvement of the subject and her community in doxastic practice. If James had been merely a precursor of these developments, he would now be of largely historical interest only. However, he was much more than a precursor. In fact his efforts were not devoted primarily to an amplification of the role of the subject in the formation of belief but to challenging the legitimacy of a point of departure for epistemology in *either* the subject *or* the world. It is the subject *and* the world which together constitute the proper starting point for epistemology, he argued in his earlier accounts of the river or stream of experience,[7] and in his later work, in Radical Empiricism, on immediate experience.

In the basic form of experience, James held, the influences involved in the intellectual life make themselves felt *together*, and while the elements of this unity are subject to retrospective, reflective disassembly, the results of such disassembly are destined to be reincorporated eventually into the unity of immediate experience where they will again exercise a mutually limiting influence upon one another. In that state they will again be put to the test by their congruence or incongruence with each other within the unity of experience as a whole, including the 'demanding context of empirically given relationships,' as McDermott put it. James's account of immediate experience is a major part of the context within which, in *The Will to Believe* and elsewhere, he commends the influence of passional nature in doxastic practice, and the persistent neglect of that context has fuelled charges of wishful thinking, charges which have thrived on the decontextualization of passional nature.

A recognition that James was not concerned exclusively with amplifying the role of the subject in doxastic practice ought to have been triggered more widely in this century by the prominent realist current which runs throughout his work. As late as 1907 he emphasized, in an interview in the *New York Times*, that while pragmatism is distinctive in its emphasis on action, 'nothing could be more ludicrous than to call this their primary interest.'[8] On the contrary, speaking in a way suggestive of a commensurateness between thought and its object which is more typical of correspondence theory than of common stereotypes of pragmatism, he claimed that 'pragmatism's primary interest is in its doctrine of truth. All pragmatist writers make this the centre of their speculations; not one of them is sceptical, not one doubts our ultimate ability to penetrate theoretically in to the very core of reality.'[9] He refers to himself in *Essays on Radical Empiricism* as a 'natural realist,'[10] and claimed earlier in *Pragmatism* that 'our true ideas of sensible things do indeed copy them. Shut your eyes and think of yonder clock on the wall, and you get just such a true picture or copy of its dial.'[11] Copying is 'primarily' a matter of 'agreement,'[12] and in what he refers to as a pivotal aspect of his position, he accepts definitions of truth and falsity which depict them as having to do with relations of agreement or disagreement which 'obtain between an idea ... and its object.'[13] The truth of conceptions 'means their "agreement," as falsity means their disagreement, with "reality."'[14] In 'The Moral Philosopher and the Moral Life' he says that 'truth supposes a standard outside of the thinker to which he must conform,'[15] and responding to critics of himself, Dewey, and Schiller, he insists that 'all three absolutely agree in admitting the transcendency of the object (provided it be an experienceable object) to the subject, in the truth-relation.'[16] Dewey, he adds, 'holds as firmly as I do to objects independent of our judgments.'

James even accepts the possibility of a proposition being absolutely true: 'On the one hand will stand reality, on the other an account of it which proves impossible to better or to alter. If the impossibility prove permanent, the truth of the account will be absolute.'[17] Such a state is 'that ideal vanishing-point towards which we imagine that all our temporary truths will some day converge.'[18] It is not clear that James viewed such a vanishing point as simply a useful fiction, a carrot at the end of the philosophical stick to keep the process of truth-seeking from becoming exhausted by its own interminability. 'Truth with a big T, and in the singular' in pragmatism's conception of it, he says, 'claims abstractly to be recognized.'[19]

One finds language throughout James's work to the effect that 'all our truths are beliefs about "Reality," and in any particular belief the reality acts as something independent, as a thing *found*, not manufactured.'[20] It is found partly through perception, through the 'flux of sensations which are forced upon us, coming we know not whence. Over their nature, order and quantity we have as good as no control.'[21] What is given in them is a 'reality "independent" of human thinking.' Such a given can be felt, often with great force, in the concrete contact with physical objects, or even according to James's ethical writings, in the historical experience of different moral relationships among human beings,[22] as we will see. In the face of such a given, many intellectual possibilities will be 'decisively rebuked.'[23]

There has been much controversy in epistemology regarding the notion of a 'given,' as James acknowledged long before more recent work by Sellars and others. Schiller and Dewey, he observes for example, understand it 'as a limit,'[24] while the scholastics understand it through the category of substance. Others 'may think to get at it in its independent nature, by peeling off the successive man-made wrappings.'[25] Henri Bergson and like-minded spirits 'bravely try to define'[26] it, while others 'say there is no core, the finally completed wrapping being reality and truth in one,' a position with which James is clearly uncomfortable.[27]

James himself is typically open in principle to this range of options. The one which is in fact correct, he says, will eventually carry the day. His own position in the interim, however, is clear. There is 'a non-human element' which one can 'know.'[28] Such knowledge, however, is not direct. The given which informs experience is only encountered in an '*imagined* aboriginal presence' (emphasis added); something that 'we may glimpse ...

but ... never grasp'[29] apart from its employment, and the success or failure to which its employment gives rise in concrete relationships with the world. What is invented allows for a recognition of what is not invented, some aspect of the world itself which has been present all along but has gone unrecognized. 'The abrupt transitions in Shakespeare's thought astonish the reader by their unexpectedness no less than they delight him by their fitness.'[30]

There is throughout James's work, then, a realist strand which ought to have raised a more widespread questioning of subjectivistic stereotypes of James's position, stereotypes which unfortunately continue to be propagated.[31] For James, 'there is something in every experience that escapes our arbitrary control. If it be sensible experience it coerces our attention; if a sequence, we cannot invert it; if we compare two terms we can come to only one result. There is a push, an urgency, within our very experience, against which we are on the whole powerless, and which drives us in a direction that is the destiny of our belief.'[32]

There is, in other words, a widely encountered recalcitrance in experience, notwithstanding the affective and intellectually creative forces which may be brought to bear upon it in an effort to shape it in self-interested ways. For James, 'reason is not the original architect of the world in which we live. There is a prior world of existence with which we are directly acquainted. Reason may take over this foundation, reform it, and build upon it. But in order to do this effectively, it must first accept it, and understand it as it is.'[33] Facts, in other words, 'are the bounds of human knowledge, set for it, not by it.'

Even Bertrand Russell acknowledged the invocation by James of 'a basis of "fact" for ... creative activity to work upon.'[34] However, he did not pursue the point vigorously enough. Had he done so, he would have better appreciated James's unification of the conceptually inventive 'building upon' what is found in the world, and the 'finding' which such building upon involves. These two activities stand in a mutually limiting tension from which neither can break entirely free. This tension is a crucial part of Radical Empiricism's account of immediate experience and provides a context in which passional nature is not at liberty to exert its influence unimpeded. The relationship between subject and world involves a *'double* intentionality,'[35] as Wild has aptly called it. The self 'not only projects intentional meanings towards others, but also receives them from others and responds to them.'[36] While it is true, in other words, that we 'humanly make an addition to ... sensible reality,' it is no less the case that 'that reality tolerates the addition'[37] in some cases and not in others. Certain additions, in this sense, '"agree" with the reality; they fit it, while they build it out.'[38] While we are at liberty to build out an understanding of the world, a trunk without a tag is not a horse, and a dog without a collar is not a tree. The world will not 'tolerate' the application of certain renderings of it, to use James's language. The 'blooming buzzing confusion' that is the world is not the unmitigated chaos which citations of that famous phrase seem most often invoked to convey. The world independent of the knower, rather, 'has germs of meaning in it, which may be developed and amplified.'[39]

This reciprocity of influence between world and knower allows for an ongoing process in which 'by a new use of language and concepts, working in cooperation with sense and feeling ... [the experiencer] will try to *find and to create* meanings that will clarify and do justice to the facts' (emphasis added).[40] While experience, for James, then, 'is not independent of our activity,'[41] as Seigfried put it in her extensive inquiries into this aspect of James's thought, it nevertheless 'includes both something given and something taken.'[42] As Edie has said, 'James is not an empirio-criticist but an *intuitionist* and what is *given* in intuitive experience is the *real* world.'[43]

The foregoing relationship which James intended be understood as existing between the creative contribution to experience by the subject, and the contribution by the world, has often been construed in a phenomenalistic vein which misleadingly separates the aboriginal occurrence of contact with the world from the conceptual organization of that contact, and sees that relationship as involving the superimposition of a conceptual system on a more basic, primitive aconceptual contact with the world.[44] A phenomenalistic understanding of James misses the most important aspect of his account: the *inseparability*, in immediate experience, of contact with the world, and the organization of this contact. Immediate experience is not an aconceptual phenomenon on which concepts and intentions are imposed; it is a conceptually *in-formed* encounter with the world. Concepts function *within* immediate experience, not just through a retrospective reflection upon it. 'Pure experience was intended [by James] to include concepts as well as percepts,'[45] Myers has accurately pointed out. In such experience there is a unity of 'space, time, conjunctive relations, change, activity ... conceiving, imagining, and remembering,'[46] sensory influences, and much else.

Hume's impressions and ideas, then, may be the most basic building blocks of experience *as reflected upon*, but, James cautions, if in a rigorously – radically – empirical manner we begin our analysis of experience by retrospectively examining the form in which it actually occurs, such impressions and ideas reveal themselves to be abstractions of fuller experiences which are more basic, experiences in which relations, intentions, concepts, dispositions, and so forth are aboriginally and seamlessly already interwoven.[47]

James's understanding of what would constitute *epistemically basic beliefs* is deeply indebted to his account of immediate experience. The most aboriginal level of experience is pure experience in its immediacy, and this experience is not compartmentalized but is a unity of many elements which make themselves felt simultaneously, and exercise a mutually limiting influence in relation to one another.[48]

One of the corollaries of James's account of immediate experience is that experience at this level cannot be made an object of direct, introspective analysis. While one can retrospectively structure previous occurrences of it, immediate experience in its transitive immediacy and unity cannot be made an object of analytic reflection. The various stages of lighting a match, for example – scraping it against the side of the box, hearing the hiss of the combustion, holding it at a distance while it flares – can be identified as distinct stages of a process in retrospect, but the actual event as an occurrence within the overall flow of experience has no such stages. In a letter to Maxwell Savage in

1910, James emphasized his indebtedness to Bergson for clarifying this for him, for showing him the extent to which 'antinomies and puzzles all come from a misapplication of concepts to the immediate flow of sensible experience.'[49]

Recognizing the elusiveness of immediate experience to direct introspective reflection, Charlene Seigfried has characterized the notion of immediate experience as a 'limit-concept,'[50] by which she means an 'explanatory hypothesis which can be postulated but not experienced as such.' Thus, 'it is never immediately experienced and communicated as such because as soon as anyone is conscious in a human sense, he has already structured that consciousness according to conceptual and verbal categories.'[51] The basic immediate relation between the subject and the world is an unanalysable relation, and here the complex unity of intellectual and non-intellectual components of experience, which I endeavoured to illustrate in the last chapter, reveals itself with particular force. Passional nature is only one of many elements of such a unity.

James's earlier efforts to develop an account of immediate experience which would preserve the double intentionality of the relation between subject and world, without lapsing into a problematic dualism of given and concept, continued in his later works. He wanted to 'retain the commonsense belief in ordinary realities (trees, human bodies) while metaphysically analyzing those realities such that their apparent boundaries disappear into a fluid continuity'[52] of actual experience. For James, however, 'boundaries meant chasms, breaks, and interruptions ... When things are identified by boundaries, they are entities, objects, or substances that involve discontinuity.'[53] Such discontinuity needed, he thought, to be reconciled with the seamless continuity which characterizes the actual flow of immediate experience. He therefore attempted to accommodate, within the continuity of immediate experience, what he thought of as its distinctive 'drops,' 'steps,' or 'pulses.' While his efforts to do this sometimes had a Berkeleyan flavour, he was not entirely Berkeleyan in his account of what actually constitutes 'the nature of the realities that exist beyond any experience. He was not prepared to follow Berkeley in preserving their existence through a godly percipient, nor was he satisfied to call them permanent possibilities of perception, as Mill did.'[54]

His position remained incomplete at the time of his death, and the question of how concepts may be included within immediate experience, 'remains a puzzle in the Jamesean metaphysis.'[55] It is a matter, however, with which James continued to struggle throughout his later works. In his analysis of the relation between percept and concept in *Some Problems of Philosophy*, for instance, the interdependence of the two, notwithstanding the distinctive contribution by each to experience, is unmistakeable. Concepts and percepts

are made of the same kind of stuff, and melt into each other when we handle them together. How could it be otherwise when the concepts are like evaporations out of the bosom of perception, into which they condense again whenever practical service summons them? No one can tell, of the things he now holds in his hand and reads, how much comes in through his eyes and fingers, and how much, from his apperceiving intellect, unites with that and makes of it this particular 'book.' The universal and the particular parts of the experience are literally immersed in each other, and both are indispensable. Conception is not like a painted hook, on which no real chain can be hung; for we hang concepts upon percepts, and percepts upon concepts interchangeably and indefinitely; and the relation of the two is much more like what we find in those cylindrical 'panoramas' in which a painted background continues a real foreground so cunningly that one fails to detect the joint.[56]

While we are able to disentangle the two to some degree through introspection, it remains the case overall that they 'play into each other's hands. Perception awakens thought, and thought in turn enriches perception. The more we see, the more we think; while the more we think, the more we see in our immediate experiences, and the greater grows the detail, and the more significant the articulateness of our perception.'[57]

James's progress in developing an account of immediate experience prior to his death can be better appreciated by considering its indebtedness to one particular image. As Myers pointed out, many major advances in the history of philosophy have involved a thinker being initially seized by a picture which so captivates the imagination that subsequent analyses become devoted to working out in detail the theoretical potential of such a picture. The picture which was deeply involved in James's struggle to develop an account of immediate experience was the picture of a mosaic. In James's case it might be more appropriate to speak about the picture in terms of metaphor, in keeping with the centrality of metaphor in his understanding of rationality.

The quest for theory is rooted in an often fortuitous, insightful *aperçu*, in which one relates formerly unrelated elements of experience, and then undertakes an exploration of the susceptibility of this relation to being developed fruitfully into theory, with empirical support. As Charlene Seigfried put it, James sought to 'combine the notion of careful and exact observation, which is characteristic of the natural sciences, with observation as romantic vision, the act of "seeing into" as practised by Emerson, Tennyson, Whitman and his other favourite poets.'[58] For James, in other words, 'the rare ability "to seize fresh aspects in concrete things" is inextricably perceptive and inventive at the same time and characterizes the great scientist as well as the great artist.'[59]

James's attention was seized so powerfully by the potential of a metaphorical juxtaposition of the field of awareness with a mosaic work of art that his pursuit of a coherent theory of immediate experience was extensively guided by that metaphor. It is one thing to come into possession of such a metaphorical *aperçu*, however, but it is another to discover whether it can provide the basis for the development of a viable philosophical theory. That process of development takes time and experiment, as was the case with James's attempt to develop the mosaic metaphor of immediate experience into a theoretical account of such experience.

It is true that James's thought about immediate experience changed in his later work. Emphasizing his philosophical kinship with Bergson, he sometimes seems in his later works to have increasingly amplified the distorting effect of conceptualization. This 'newly aggressive radical empiricism'[60] was subjected to criticism by Dickinson Miller and Arthur Lovejoy, among others, as too indiscriminate in its attack on conceptualization. 'Miller seems to have been quite fair in his suggestion that James should have confined his protest to those concepts that imply that there is more discreteness and lack of movement in the perceptually given than is actually to be found there.'[61]

Myers' judgment of James's later work on the unity of immediate experience is more deeply critical, notwithstanding Myers' keen appreciation of and sympathy for James's aims. James backed himself into what Myers considers to have been an untenable position in a way which can be illustrated by invoking the basic metaphor of the mosaic. Unlike the mosaic piece of art, the pieces of the mosaic of immediate experience, as James envisioned it, are related not as discrete entities cemented into a common bedding but are related at their 'edges' by their *relations* with other elements of the field of experience. Setting aside the problems involved in James's argument that the relations among the parts of the experiential field may themselves be discrete objects of experience, we can turn our attention to the way in which the problem of immediate experience presented itself to James within such relational terms of reference.

In an attempt to better accommodate the individuality and recalcitrance of some aspects of immediate experience, without undermining the seamlessness of experience as a whole, James developed his mosaic image in a way which portrayed the elements of experience as overlapping so that they could be thought of as merging into one another in a borderless fashion, as it were, without entirely forfeiting their autonomy. One might in this connection envision a watercolour painting in which the various colours, while distinct, have been allowed to flow into each other so that there are no clearly definable lines of demarcation among them. Myers effectively characterizes both the metaphysical and epistemological aspects of such a position in describing James as having held that

contiguity, adjacency, or what he often referred to as nextness is a datum for direct apprehension which can be assumed to exist throughout the universe such that any given experience or thing is connected by a series of contiguous intermediaries to any other experience or thing. The universe is not merely a disconnected assemblage of processes but is rather a concatenation or mosaic of pluralistic items. It has the continuity of nextness between things, which yields a degree of unity ... We can view the plural realities as accessible to each other by connecting paths, flowings of the sort that we know in our own steams of consciousness.[62]

As Myers points out, however, among the obstacles which lay in the path of developing a theory along these lines was the contention, which James had proposed in his early thought, that mental states can not be compounded. The identity of a particular mental state, for James, lay 'in its indivisible unity or ... unanalyzable awareness.'[63] A development of the mosaic image which, in the interests of doing justice to the unity of immediate experience, would involve the 'inclusion of one mental state within another in a successive series,'[64] would seem to require the compounding of mental states. A discrete aspect of experience, however, could not be seen as overlapping with, and becoming sufficiently part of another – in order to sustain the continuity of experience – without such being-a-part-of compromising the indivisibility and autonomy of the units involved. 'A unit cannot be indivisible and at the same time include another unit, nor can it owe its identity simultaneously to being indivisible and to being part of a larger unit. These contradictions resulted from the admission that mental states can include each other.'[65]

The die was cast with respect to immediate experience, in Myers's judgment, by James's concession of the compounding of mental states.

James believed that nothing remained but to surrender any further attempts to talk coherently about the identity of the mental states that constitute the flow of pure experience. To abandon the original idea that mental states are units would have denied James the means of identifying any mental state. Without their nature as units, James thought, mental states are virtually indistinguishable, and we have lost the logic of identity.[66]

In Myers's view, then, James ultimately came to see himself as being forced into the adoption of irrationalism. 'When everything is reduced to a phase of the flux of pure experience, as in the Jamesian pluralistic universe, then things have a very slippery identity indeed. Sounding somewhat like Hegel, he remarked in *A Pluralistic Universe*: "It is that there is a sense in which real things are not merely their own selves, but they may vaguely be treated as also their own others, and that ordinary logic, since it denies this, must be overcome."'[67]

Myers acknowledges the efforts of some commentators to anticipate how James's position might have been developed in an less irrationalist direction if he had lived longer. Myers gives a sympathetic hearing, for example, to Perry's suggestion that James might well have developed a view according to which the elements which stand out within the flow of experience could be characterized as 'ephemeral specious presents [which] are the basic units of our experience and can be thought of as phases or pulses that retain at least a momentary identity before being changed by the experiential flux of which they are a part. Continuity results if these minimal pulses of reality are considered the finite components of growing processes like motion and change ... finite drops, buds or steps.'[68] James proposed these components as constitutive of immediate experience. The problems occasioned by James's later decision to allow for the compounding of states of consciousness, however, in Myers's judgment, made it 'impossible to follow Perry's recipe for dissolving the dilemma.'[69] In the end, 'the pure experience concept did not permit clear distinction between the objective and subjective dimensions of a conscious state.'[70] James's efforts to impute objectivity and subjectivity to a more fundamental phenomenon, pure experience, did not work out. 'This Jamesian contention only confuses us because we can never find an *it* that is sometimes a stable pen and at other times an instable awareness of a pen ... It is questionable whether a world in which mental and physical things abruptly exchange identities is intelligible, but such a world clearly cannot be used for explaining the world we experience.'[71]

There certainly is textual support for Myers's criticisms. 'I went through the inner catastrophe,' James admits with respect to his work on immediate experience. 'I was bankrupt intellectually, and had to change my base ... If any of you try sincerely and pertinaciously on your own separate accounts to intellectualize reality, you may be similarly driven to a change of front.'[72] He abandoned the notion that states of consciousness cannot be compounded, as I indicated above;[73] he amplified his allegiance to Bergson; he underscored the degree to which the apparently discrete aspects of experience are 'their own others,'[74] and he widened the gap between pure experience and conceptualization.[75]

On the other hand, however, even in his late work, James claims that the religiosity of his mature humanism is 'susceptible of a reasoned defense,'[76] a position which certainly seems to be at odds with irrationalism and with the fideistic religiosity which would appear to be an unavoidable corollary of irrationalism. He anticipated Myers's objection that we cannot reflectively isolate an 'it' which counts twice as subjective and objective, saying forthrightly that 'there is no *general* stuff of which experience at large is made.[77] The objective and subjective modes of appearance are *events* involved in actual commerce with the world. 'Knowledge of sensible realities ... comes to life inside the tissue of experience. It is *made*; and made by relations that unroll themselves in time.[78]

There is much in James's later work on immediate experience, moreover, to suggest that he did not intend to give up on the double intentionality of his earlier thought in favour of an irrationalistic abandonment of conceptualization, but intended rather to develop his earlier position more deeply. When he recalls, as seen above for example, that he had been compelled eventually to 'change base' with respect to conceptualization, he adds that this had been a movement away from attempts to 'intellectualize reality,'[79] and there is much in his attacks on rationalism in related texts which suggests that what James was resisting was the wholesale imperviousness, in the intellectualizing propensities of many rationalists, to the vagaries of the *particular* – to the ever reappearing 'novelty' which James congratulates Pierce for having emphasized.[80]

Moreover, when he commends the heraclitean element of Bergson's thought, he does so with the provision that Bergson's repudiation of logic is a repudiation of the notion that 'in the actual world the logical axioms hold good *without qualification*' (emphasis added).[81] What is more, as Hare has pointed out, James's later work moves in an irrationalist and fideistic direction only 'intermittently.'[82] In addition, there are a number of signs that the later essays resist a wholesale irrationalism. In *A Pluralistic Universe*, for example, there are indications of a more moderate position. On the one hand, it is true, as Myers points out, that James says 'the gist of the matter is always the same – something ever goes indissolubly with something else. You cannot separate the same from its other, except by abandoning the real altogether and taking to the conceptual system. What is immediately given in the single and particular instance is always something pooled and mutual.'[83] James goes on, however, to add that 'no one elementary bit of reality is eclipsed from the next bit's point of view, if only we take reality sensibly and in small enough pulses.' As Hare notes, in the Appendix to *A Pluralistic Universe*, 'James does not so much say that concepts falsify the present perceptual flux as that changing reality must be constantly reconceptualized to capture novelties. This suggests that fundamentally James did not wish to discredit all conceptual thinking but only to encourage the development of more flexible thinking.'[84]

Assertions by James, then, to the effect that "sensational experiences *are* their "own others,"' while supporting the contention that he had abandoned the logic of identity, must be taken alongside additional assertions to the effect that notwithstanding such interrelations, the discreteness of the parts of experience, and its recalcitrance in many instances, are not wholly lost. Taken together, such assertions support claims by Hare and others that, in the later stages of James's struggle to produce a viable account of immediate experience which unites subject and world without forfeiting the double intentionality of that relation, he was not embracing a wholesale irrationalism but sought to overcome the limits of conceptualization through a more inventive use of conceptualization itself:

Although Bergson's anti-intellectualism doubtless led James to an overzealous attack on the discrete and the static, James's recognition of the reality of continuity in the perceptual flux was a fundamental insight that antedated by decades his contact with Bergson. His problem, which he did not live to solve, was to invent *concepts* that would fairly capture, without self-contradiction, both the continuity and the discreteness of the perceptual flux.[85]

With respect to his later struggles with the notion of immediate experience, then, it can be argued that James was exploring the limits of, rather than entirely abandoning, the logic of identity, and that he was doing so in the pursuit of a level of conceptual creativity which would preserve the double intentionality of immediate, concrete experience in all its complex dynamism and recalcitrance.

A clear resolution of the differences among the positions of Myers, Hare, and others regarding James's successes and failures in preserving the double intentionality of immediate experience in his later work remains to be worked out completely. A further detailed pursuit of that issue at this point is beyond the range of my project. What I have attempted to establish is that the context for the functioning of passional nature in James's epistemology and philosophy of religion is immediate experience as a whole, and that passional nature must function in concert with many other elements which together constitute such experience. Charges against James throughout this century for wishful thinking overwhelmingly ignore this major aspect of his thought and so ignore the many elements which restrict the scope of influence of passional nature. I propose, in this light, that analysts abandon the perennial rehearsals of wishful thinking charges, and turn the focus of their inquiries regarding James's philosophy of religion towards a careful analysis of immediate experience, for immediate experience furnishes the context for James's thought on belief formation and religion, and the role of passional nature in these areas.

Among the results of a deeper appreciation of the context which James's thought on immediate experience provides for his epistemology and his philosophy of religion, would be a better understanding of his recourse to consequences in the adjudication of truth, including the consequences of theism which have been widely touted as prudentially motivating the adoption of theistic belief where such belief does not already exist. While unanalysable in its immediacy, immediate experience can be subject to indirect scrutiny through reflection on the concrete relations with the world to which it gives rise, and this is why James appeals to the personal responses of the subject – to satisfaction, utility and profitability – in connection with truth. When he includes satisfaction among the consequences of holding a particular view, for example, it is not just personal satisfaction that he is talking about, but the fulfilment or disappointment of expectations about the world, about an anticipated 'fit' between thought and world which may or may not have actually developed in the course of immediate experience as a whole. 'As Chisholm and other critics have pointed out, James did not mean by the satisfactoriness of a theory that it would satisfy certain subjective desires, as certain European critics have maintained. He meant rather its capacity to satisfy certain expectations'[86] about the world.

> Any meaning ultimately points to a reality in some region of the world which is supposed to bear this meaning. If I move by appropriate actions in this direction, and, by a continuous series of steps, finally find myself in the vicinity of a real being which I then find by direct perception, feeling, and response, to have this meaning, it is verified. If, on the other hand, my steps are interrupted by unbridgeable discontinuities and chasms which separate me from the assumed reality, then the meaning is not an adequate guide, and is disconfirmed. Thus if, in reaching for the black pen I seem to see before me, my hand encounters a solid pane of glass separating me from it, my belief was really mistaken, and I was probably seeing only a reflection of the pen.[87]

The same holds true of 'profitability' language. 'By "most profitable" James does not mean an isolated, subjective feeling of "profit" or "satisfaction" that is not a satisfaction in something. The true idea is profitable in enabling me to orient myself properly in dealing with real beings independent of me.'[88]

This position does not preclude a serious pursuit of objectivity but gives that pursuit real substance:

> The pragmatic position that concrete truth for us will always be that way of thinking in which our various experiences most profitably combine provides as sure a foothold for nonarbitrary truth as can be provided by any believer in an independent realm of reality. The concrete conditions under which our thinking actually takes place do not permit us to play fast and loose with the order in which experiences come to us without suffering the consequences. And those who appeal to a non-experimental basis for their truth claims, such as is implied in the correspondence formula, are making idle statements of no help in determining any actual truth. Such an empty formula becomes meaningful only insofar as its stated relation of subject to predicate can be shown to be operative within the leading of finite experiences, in which case it is no longer a mere correspondence but the actual working out of 'a leading that is worthwhile.' Objectivity and independence in truth, instead of being undermined by the pragmatic insistence on the irreducibly human component of truth, actually receive their first clear explanation and verifiable support.[89]

This is not a position which so deeply severs the subject from the world that she can indefinitely and with impunity name as 'true' anything which pleases her, as Russell, Myers, Pojman, and others have charged. It is a position, rather, which attempts to do justice to both the 'unanalysable' relation with the world in immediate experience, and to the capacity to reflect on that relation after it has transpired, to consult its consequences, and interpret the significance of those consequences. It is a position which involves a push and pull among personal interests, the 'inward necessity' of conceptual systems, the 'resistance' or accommodation by the world of interests and systems in immediate experience, and the subject's response to that relation in reflection.

*Within* this constellation of influences, facticity and objectivity are both meaningful and important, and James repeatedly affirms their importance. 'When as empiricists we give up the doctrine of objective certitude,' he says in *The Will to Believe*, for example, 'we do not thereby give up the quest or hope of truth itself,'[90] and, in the main thesis statement of that essay, he asserts, in connection with religion, that indefinitely awaiting evidence has the same risk of losing the '*truth*' as proceeding without decisive evidence. Religious propositions are said to be potentially 'true,' 'right' and subject to assessment according to 'evidence.'[91] He also qualifies his endorsement of risk in religious belief by saying that what he has in mind is 'the risk of acting as if my passional need of taking the world religiously might be prophetic and *right*' (emphasis added),[92] as he puts it analogously in the case of morality. Such allegiance to objectivity is echoed implicitly in the negative vocabulary with which he speaks, in *The Will to Believe* and elsewhere, in connection with purely idiosyncratic convictions, for he warns against the risk of inadvertently embracing propositions on the basis of '*il*legitimate cravings.' His comments to Mark Baldwin to the effect that observers restrain themselves from judging the integrity of another's beliefs because of the difficulty of determining the measure of the believer's sincerity and evidence presuppose James's expectation that the individual will pursue such sincerity and evidence in her own intellectual practices.

In his correspondence, James again indicates that he is anxious to dispel any impression that he is condoning beliefs which have no warrant beyond the wishes of the believer. Writing to Mark Baldwin, he strongly rejects any relation between his essay and 'a man pretending to himself to believe what he does n't [sic] believe,'[93] or between the essay and beliefs embraced in wilful stubbornness. In a letter to Ralph Barton Perry, he objects strenuously to the notion that satisfaction of desire as such is somehow the *sine qua non* of the determination of truth.

> You speak ... as if the 'degree of satisfaction' was *exclusive* of theoretic satisfactions. Who ever said or implied this? Surely neither Dewey, Schiller nor I have ever denied that sensation, relation, and funded truth 'dispose,' in their measure, of what we 'pro-

pose.' Nothing that we propose can violate them; but *they satisfied*, what *in addition* gratifies our aesthetic or utilitarian demands best will always be counted as *more* true. My position is that, *other things equal*, emotional satisfactions count for truth – among the other things being the intellectual satisfactions.[94]

It is a misrepresentation of James, then, to suggest that the prominent role in his epistemology of human inventiveness and personal influence leads necessarily to a field-day for wishful thinking, for the exercise of these elements is circumscribed in many important ways.

It is, of course, true that the various components which are unified in immediate experience can be pulled far apart in reflective activity. We are capable of standing back from immediate experience and manipulating it in an enormous variety of ways. These can range from the tentative hypotheses of the scientist to the body-image of the anorexic adolescent. Such developments may be blatantly self-serving, even delusional. There is no question about our ability to manipulate experience in self-interested and imaginative ways, as James the psychologist knew better than most philosophers.

Such inventive machinations cannot be separated indefinitely, however, from living; they cannot be preserved indefinitely, that is, from their eventual reintegration into the immediate experience of either the individual or her community in which once again 'the act-content-object distinction ... collapses into content alone.'[95] This collapse yields precisely the characteristic of immediate experience which James emphasizes as being its most important characteristic: the *unification* of concept, world, and subject, a unification which will give rise to successful or unsuccessful relationships with the world. Subjective influences, then, may for a period of time, or in a particular individual or community, be accorded a degree of autonomy which is able to distort belief. In the long run, however, the incompatibility of these distortions with the other aspects of the field of immediate experience into which those distortions will eventually be concretely reintegrated, will expose such distortions for what they are. The largely ahistorical and individualistic character of much epistemology in this century has occasioned a serious neglect of these crucial aspects of James's position, for the adjudication of experience is ultimately a collective and historical process.

It is difficult to formulate a description of James's position which does justice to its realist component without at the same time undermining its pragmatic character. Carlos Prado's characterization of Dewey's thought, in contrast to Rorty's, is serviceable in this connection. Like Dewey, James holds that with 'enough success and consistency in practice and prediction, a theoretical application works as it does because it *gets things right.*'[96] That is to say,

> the best use of intelligence – disciplined and cooperative inquiry – must eventually achieve truth, in the sense that inquiry will result in practices of such efficacy and stability that we can only judge them so because of correctness. Inquiry may not achieve Cartesian certainty, but, always allowing that we might be wrong, it will achieve success explicable only in terms of descriptive correctness. And if we decide we are wrong at any point, it will be that are *wrong*, not that we have abandoned one story for one we like better.[97]

Prado here locates 'efficacy' exactly where James located it, in the context of an ongoing historical dialectic between intelligent reflection and immediate experience. While realist in its own way, James's position is neither conventionally realist nor idealist. His agenda, rather, was to find 'a way out of this sterile impasse [between realism and idealism] ... As Ralph Barton Perry has pointed out, with great penetration, the philosophy of James is neither a philosophy of objects and actions nor a philosophy of ideas; it is a philosophy of the experience of objects and actions in which the subject itself is a participant. The root of James's pragmatism lies here.'[98]

It is true, notwithstanding this, that in many respects, as I pointed out, there is what James calls a 'looseness' in our relationship with the world. While aware 'that heat melts ice, that salt preserves meat, that fish die out of water,'[99] and 'sure that fire will burn and water wet us,'[100] we are 'less sure that thunder will come after lightning, [and] not at all sure whether a strange dog will bark at us or let us go by.'[101] Such uncertainty increases in other domains. 'Though nature's materials lend themselves slowly and discouragingly to our translation of them into ethical forms, but more readily into aesthetic forms; to translation into scientific forms they lend themselves with relative ease and completeness. The translation, it is true, will probably never be ended. The perceptive order does not give way, nor the right conceptive substitute for it arise, at our bare word of command.'[102] James might as readily have added that 'nature's materials lend themselves slowly and discouragingly to our translation of them' into religious categories also, and what he proposes in his philosophy of religion is proposed within these terms of reference. James's comments in this respect are reminiscent of C.D. Broad's in a similar connection:

> It is worth while to remember that modern science has almost as humble an ancestry as contemporary religion. If the primitive witch-smeller is the spiritual progenitor of the Archbishop of Canterbury, the primitive rain-maker is equally the spiritual progenitor of the Cavendish Professor of Physics. There has obviously been a gradual refinement and purification of religious beliefs and concepts in the course of history, just as there has been in the beliefs and concepts of science ... It seems somewhat arbitrary to count this process as a continual approximation to true knowledge of the material aspect of the world in the case of science, and to refuse to regard it as at all similar in the case of religion.[103]

Given the foregoing 'looseness,' it is not entirely clear what to make of the distinctive states characterizing live theism. Live theism, as I pointed out, is, according to *The Will to Believe*, experienced by many people as rooted tenaciously in the 'heart,' the 'instincts,'[104] 'good-will,'[105] and even human nature itself, and seems to call for a benefit of the doubt which would not be responsible in all cases of discursive inquiry. It also involves a distinctive noetic element, an intellectual broadening and personal invigoration described as the strenuous mood, as will be seen in the next chapter.

However, such states do not stand alone. They stand, within immediate experience, alongside additional 'empirically given relationships' with the world with which they seem on many counts to be congruent. They also, however, stand alongside other aspects of the world involving evil and suffering, for example, with which they do not seem to be congruent. James willingly admits that in many of its common forms, dogmatic theism seems to be irreconcilable with these latter features of the world. He readily concedes, in *The Varieties of Religious Experience*, that he does not know exactly what theological form theism would have to take in order to respond adequately to such incongruities, although he makes some tentative suggestions, including the attribution of finitude to the deity.

Experience as a whole, in other words, is a mixed bag. The distinctive characteristics of live theism are framed, returning to McDermott's point, by a diversity of other experiences which preclude either an unqualified acceptance of dogmatic theism, as it is currently received in the Christian West at least, or an unqualified dismissal of it as projection. James nowhere says or even suggests that the decision to acquiesce in an existing theistic propensity makes the 'threatening' alternatives go away. On the contrary, the direction of his position, as I have depicted it, is to sustain a dialectical relation between live theism and the considerations by which such a theism is 'threatened,' a tension which James is eager to sustain because it is only the pursuit of its resolution which will gradually expose the viability or lack of viability of received theisms or atheisms.

Human beings will, of course, vary in their ability and willingness to discern the intellectual significance of the tensions within immediate experience as a whole, in this respect or in others, and this leaves plenty of room for wishful thinking. There is nothing in James's corpus, however, which would suggest that he intended to encourage the exploitation of this for the purpose of gratifying self-deception. He was realistic enough, nevertheless, to understand that any workable epistemology would have to acknowledge the scope for distortion which is made available by the capacity to reflectively disassemble immediate experience, reconstitute it to one's self-serving advantage, and ignore some of the perplexing results of such reconstitution in subsequent immediate experience. There is no 'rule of thinking' such as Clifford's which can eliminate the exploitation of that latitude where there is a will to do so.

A crucial aspect of the intellectual life, James realized, therefore, must be accorded to the irreplaceability of a role for the subject as subject, for a personal willingness to work hard and honestly at recognizing the lessons about certain concepts which emerge from the experiential consequences of integrating those concepts into immediate experience. This aspiration to discernment will emerge as particularly important in the next chapter. Such aspiration involves volition, personal integrity, emotional maturity, character and other such subjective influences. It is for this reason, among others, that James urges an inclusion of these influences in epistemology, and one is reminded of certain strands of contemporary virtue epistemology in this connection.[106]

Choice, personal integrity, emotional maturity, character and other elements are integrated by James into epistemology, then, precisely in order to *curtail* wishful thinking, and promote objectivity in belief, contrary to the burden of critical literature which depicts these elements as opening the door to such abuses. If immediate experience cannot be directly reflected upon, and its consequences are not self-interpreting, then intellectual progress is dependent on such human attributes, and on a willingness on the part of the individual and the community to undertake an honest discernment of the ways in which current thought may, as James was seen previously to have put it, 'violate the character with which life concretely comes and the expression which it bears of being, or at least of involving, a muddle and struggle, with an "ever not quite" to all our formulas, and novelty and possibility forever leaking in.'[107]

Sound intellectual progress is dependent on the acceptance by individuals of personal responsibility for attending closely to *all* the relevant consequences of their beliefs, and here I underscore once again this chapter's emphasis on the overall unity of experience. It is many of James's commentators, not James, who compartmentalize the many influences which 'really do produce our creeds' in a way which leads to much greater autonomy for subjective influences than they actually possess in the position of James himself. In his accounts of both the stream of experience and immediate experience, James seeks to block such compartmentalization as well as the autonomy which would be given to subjective influences within the terms of reference of such a compartmentalization.

Alongside whatever personal edification some people may derive from a doctrine of papal infallibility, to take up one of Russell's examples, one must also consult intellectual consequences as well, as James emphasized in correspondence with Perry. One such intellectual consequence of claims to papal infallibility might involve the 14th century Avignon papacy during which there were three popes who were proposing mutually exclusive teachings on some important matters, and even excommunicating each other. This historical state of affairs stands in stark contrast with an unqualified imputation of infallibility to the papacy. One of the consequences of holding that the pope is infallible under all circumstances, in other words, is the advent of a blatant conflict with what is known about the Avignon papacy, and insofar as belief in such infallibility occasions such conflict, it does not pay; it does not work. That is to say, one of the *consequences* of subscribing to a simplistic notion of papal infallibility is the generating of an intractable intellectual conflict between two contentions. It is precisely such a conflict to which a foe of papal infallibility such as Russell would himself presumably call attention in an inquiry aimed at trying 'to settle the plain question of fact' about this doctrine.

There is nothing in James's position to suggest that the emotional satisfaction which some people seem to derive from being led authoritatively by a person who is purportedly inerrant is in any way more important in the pursuit of facticity than is the foregoing conflict. Both are consequences, and James's position does not allow for either to be ignored. The failure of an unqualified doctrine of papal infallibility to square with the Avignon papacy would signal the strong possibility that the positive affective responses engendered among some people by that doctrine may reflect the intrusion of self-interest.

The same point can be applied to James's position with respect to theism. The presence of suffering and evil in the world conflicts seriously with a theism which proposes an omnipotent deity, which is why James advocated, in *The Varieties of Religious Experience*, that closer attention be given to amending conventional Christian theism to better accommodate this phenomenon.

Overall, then, the role of the subject in epistemology commended by James ought to be understood within the terms of reference of his account of immediate experience as a whole in which the many elements involved exercise a mutually restrictive role. It is not just certain subjective states *by themselves* which concern James in *The Will to Believe*, or which are thought by him to justify theism. His concern is with the significance of the ways in which the states characteristic of live theism are congruent with some aspects of immediate experience as a whole, and incongruent with others. His concern is also with the significance of those states if there is a broad commensurateness between persons and world, a topic to which I will return in the next chapter. The importance accorded to the distinctive states characteristic of live theism, then, is accorded to them by James within the context of their relations with many other aspects of the field of experience, of individuals' and communities' ongoing, concrete relations with the world. Given the many constraints involved in this context, such states do not possess the autonomy which would justify the sorts of generalized charges which have been brought perennially against James for having sponsored wishful thinking. James's account of immediate experience did remain unfinished and deficient in ways suggested earlier in this chapter. Even as it stands, however, it provides a sound philosophical basis for resisting the widespread propensity among commentators to compartmentalize experience, when analysing James, in spite of his repeated emphasis on the fundamental interrelations and interdependencies among the many elements of experience.

In sum, then, it is James's contention that while thought in many instances does not simply reproduce the world pictorially like a mirror, neither does it consist only of a sequence of Rortian stories which are appealing to the subject or the community of subjects. Passional nature is not autonomous in its prerogative of prompting one to affirm truth or falsity of any current convictions whatever, however personally attractive, although neither James nor anyone else can stop this from occurring where there is a will on the part of an individual – or sometimes even a community, as James points out in some of his stinging criticisms of American society[108] – to do so.

My portrayal of James's position, admittedly, does not lead to an unambiguous justification of theism, but that was not my intention. It was intended to attack the longstanding propensity among commentators to ignore the centrepiece of James's epistemology, the complex unity of immediate experience, and neglect therefore the degree to which, within such a position, subjective influences are integrally involved in an immediate, multi-dimensional concrete relationship with the world which issues in results and consequences that cannot be responsibly ignored, and which limit the impact of subjective influence in the formation of belief.

# 4

# The Strenuous Mood

The widespread view throughout this century that, according to James, we are entitled to believe religiously in spite of insufficient evidence has been understood primarily in two ways. The first of these is prudential. Such a choice, it is said, would give rise to certain personally desirable consequences which it would be imprudent to ignore. John Hick is one of many who read James this way, and he was sharply critical of James for holding such a position. Hick charged that the prudential argument trivializes religion by reducing it to a self-interested toss of the dice which is comparable, in Hick's judgment, to Pascal's wager.

James also justified movement ahead of adequate evidence, it is held, on the basis of the need, as in science, to pursue the truth or falsity of what he sometimes refers to as the religious 'hypothesis.' Bertrand Russell, among others, argued that this involves a confusion of belief and hypothesis-adoption. James mistakenly assumed, that is, that the permissibility of moving ahead of evidence in the case of hypothesis-adoption, in anticipation of certain as-yet-unknown consequences of inquiry, is also permissible in the domain of belief. Hypothesis-adoption, however, Russell rightly pointed out, need not necessarily involve belief.

Both of the foregoing lines of interpretation and criticism of James remain influential today, and both are seriously flawed, as I will show in this chapter. They are flawed above all by their failure to explore in detail exactly what consequences were in fact held by James to flow from live theism, and to explore the nature of the relationship between those consequences and the belief state. Had the nature of those consequences and their relation to live theism been studied more diligently over the decades commentators would have discovered that James did not hold that one ought to adopt religious belief on the basis mainly of the personally beneficial consequences to which it gives rise. Nor did he confuse belief and hypothesis-adoption in commending live theism in anticipation of its as-yet-unknown intellectual consequences.

The major consequences of theism are enumerated and described by James principally under the heading of what he calls the 'strenuous mood,' a term which is strikingly rare in the literature on James's philosophy. The neglect of this notion has been as significant in its impact on the reception of his thought as has been the neglect of liveness in the reception of *The Will to Believe*. The neglect of liveness, as I have shown, has obscured the fact that one of the main concerns of James's philosophy of religion has to do with the consequences of abandoning an existing theistic belief, or propensity to believe. The neglect of the strenuous mood, for its part, has obscured the fact that the abandonment of live theism would involve the loss of both the personal and the intellectual elements which together, and inseparably, constitute that mood. An appreciation of what such a loss entails is necessary if the aforementioned famous interpretations and criticisms of James's position are to be judged soundly.

Inquiry into what James means by the strenuous mood is best begun by turning to his account of the moral life. In 'The Moral Philosopher and the Moral Life,' his major work in ethics, he distinguishes between the 'easy-going' and the 'strenuous' moods. The ruling sentiment of the easy-going mood is 'the shrinking from present ill.'[1] The subject's ideals here are 'mere preferences of his own'[2] with which, in the interests of avoiding ill, he can 'play fast or loose ... at will.'[3] The easygoing life is not entirely bereft of moral substance on this account, but it is limited by the individual's particular interests; its range of concerns is 'played on the compass of a couple of poor octaves'[4] reflective of the subject's own particular allegiances.

The interests of other persons may be present to such a disposition but they are not as pressing as they might otherwise be. While one may profess, for example, to be solicitous of the welfare of future generations, the claims of those distant generations are not felt with as great an urgency as would be the case in the strenuous mood. This is so because those generations, like ours, along with our efforts on their behalf, are seen as ultimately destined to vanish into an anonymous 'vacuous beyond' of extinction. It is the futility of all such efforts, then, future generations' as well as our own, which dampens the eagerness to sacrifice present interests on behalf of persons yet to be born; 'no need of agonizing ourselves or making others agonize for these good creatures just at present.'[5]

When the moral order is understood as having a transcendent origin and destiny, however, the demands of that order are experienced differently, for a broader scope and permanence accrue to them. 'The scale of the symphony is incalculably prolonged. The more imperative ideals now begin to speak with an altogether new objectivity and significance, and to utter the penetrating, shattering, tragically challenging note of appeal.'[6] History bears constant testimony, James observes, to the 'antagonism of the strenuous and genial moods' in this respect; to the differences between 'the ethics of infinitude and mysterious obligation from on high, and those of prudence and the satisfaction of merely finite need.'[7] As he says in *Varieties*:

> The lustre of the present hour is always borrowed from the background of possibilities it goes with. Let our common experiences be enveloped in an eternal moral order; let our suffering have an immortal significance; let Heaven smile upon the earth, and deities pay their visits; let faith and hope be the atmosphere which man breathes in; – and his days pass by with zest; they stir with prospects, they thrill with remoter values. Place round them on the contrary the curdling cold and gloom and absence of all permanent meaning which for pure naturalism and the popular-science evolutionism of our time are all that is visible ultimately, and the thrill stops short, or turns rather to an anxious trembling.[8]

In *Essays on Faith and Morals* the same point arises, 'a nameless *unheimlichkeit* comes over us at the thought of there being nothing eternal in our final purposes, in the objects of those loves and aspirations which are our deepest energies.'[9]

The strenuous mood, then, suffuses the moral life as a whole with 'the note of infinitude and mystery.'[10] It involves, he says in connection with saintliness, 'a feeling of being in a wider life than that of this world's selfish little interests'[11] in a way which underlines the differences between the natural and the spiritual dispositions towards the world. For the former, 'the world is a sort of rectilinear or one-storied affair, whose accounts are kept in one denomination, whose parts have just the values which naturally they appear to have, and of which a simple algebraic sum of pluses and minuses will give the total worth.'[12]

To the spiritual view, the world is a 'double-storied mystery' in which 'natural good is not simply insufficient in amount and transience.' Natural good falls short of human moral aspirations for the *summum bonum* as well, James argues in a way reminiscent of Kant. The natural good, 'cancelled as it all is by death if not by earlier enemies ... gives no final balance, and can never be the thing intended for our lasting worship. It keeps us from our real good, rather; and renunciation and despair of it are our first step in the direction of the truth.'[13]

We are dealing here not only with moral sentiments and a broadening of intellectual horizons to include a transcendent, but also with distinctive forms of action which the empirical analyses of *The Varieties of Religious Experience* indicate are uniquely related to the perspective of the strenuous mood. In his preamble to the lectures on saintliness in *Varieties*, James indicates that a survey of the actual behaviour of those living in the strenuous mood is 'the pleasantest portion of our business,'[14] for here one finds that 'the best fruits of religious experience are the best things that history has to show. They have always been esteemed so.' One encounters extraordinary examples of 'charity, devotion, trust, patience, bravery,'[15] and other virtues.

The practitioner of love of one's enemy, for example, while appearing from one point of view to be the hopelessly naive and impractical 'dupe and victim of his charitable fever,'[16] bent upon a waste of time and energy, nevertheless stands apart from his warring or prudent contemporaries in one important respect. His imprudently risky and vulnerable initiatives make possible, at least, something which surpasses the potential of the use of force which destroys the enemy, or the use of prudence which protects only goods presently in hand.[17] Unlike force and prudence, such love of one's enemy can potentially produce the 'vital and essential' regenerative transformation of the enemy into a friend, and the renewal of the human community arising uniquely out of such regeneration.

Not only the enemy, but the socially disenfranchised are drawn into the moral purview of the strenuous mood as well, in James's account, furnishing further regenerative contributions to the community, as well as to individuals. The religious identification with the economic outcast, for example, has suffused 16 centuries of monastic and other forms of religious behaviour in a manner which is utterly alien to 'the way in which wealth-getting enters as an ideal into the very bone and marrow of our generation.'[18] Material self-abdication through the voluntary adoption of poverty 'is the strenuous life,'[19] James says; it is a 'moral equivalent of war'[20] which transforms the ideal of self-less heroism, traditionally associated with military risk and self-sacrifice, into a strenuous heroism of ascetic identification with the disenfranchised through the personal abdication of one's material privileges.

Throughout *The Varieties of Religious Experience*, one finds repeatedly James's illustration of direct links between religious belief and these, as well as other distinctive forms of behaviour, such as the immediate cessation of formerly intractable patterns of destructive and reprehensible activity, and the sudden acquisition of new habits which endure for a lifetime. James's empirical inquiries in this vein, and many other comparable ones independent of his, strongly suggest that in the cases recorded this behaviour would not exist apart from the live theism which appears to have precipitated it. James's study of such links between belief and the distinctive forms of behaviour which accompany it lends substance to his contention in *The Will to*

*Believe* that the abandonment of live theism would have momentous consequences at the level of action.[21]

From this initial brief foray into James's understanding of the strenuous mood, the first thing I wish to bring to prominence is that the strenuous mood is not a distinctive, affectively pleasurable state which would be worthy of pursuit on prudential grounds. It is, rather, a possible *property* that the moral life may possess, if the moral life is conducted under certain conditions. Attractive personal consequences may be involved, but they are inseparable from many other elements.

An appreciation of the unity of all such elements which constitute the moral life as a whole, and apart from which the strenuous mood cannot be properly understood, begins with a recognition of James's pronounced resistance to the domination of ethics by one particular element: *theory.* Such a domination conceals the basic nature of moral life and reflection, and obscures the contextual setting of the strenuous mood.[22] 'There is no such thing possible as an ethical philosophy dogmatically made up in advance,'[23] James argues stridently in 'The Moral Philosopher and the Moral Life.' What guides the development of the moral life is actual human demand: 'every *de facto* claim creates in so far forth an obligation,'[24] albeit only a *prima facie* one. The most basic tenet of James's moral philosophy is the contention that

the essence of good is simply to satisfy demand. The demand may be for anything under the sun. There is really no more ground for supposing that all our demands can be accounted for by one universal underlying kind of motive than there is ground for supposing that all physical phenomena are cases of a single law. The elementary forces in ethics are probably as plural as those of physics are. The various ideals have no common character apart from the fact that they are ideals. No single abstract principle can be so used as to yield to the philosopher anything like a scientifically accurate and genuinely useful casuistic scale.[25]

What legitimacy, however, could there be in the demands of a ruthless sweatshop supervisor? Such demands have no legitimacy, James would be quick to affirm, but he is particularly eager to emphasize the importance of recognizing why this is so. The answer brings to the fore a distinctive relationship between demand and theory which lies at the centre of James's ethical thought. He does not want to eliminate moral theory altogether. Instead, he wants to hold it in a certain tension with the actual historical processes from which he recognizes that it arises, and to which he understands it to be perpetually indebted. This twinning of the theoretical and the concrete in James's ethical thought ought not to come as any surprise. It is simply another manifestation of the dialectic between the theoretical and the concrete which, as I have emphasized, is the hallmark of Radical Empiricism in all areas of inquiry.

Moral theory, for James, is a reflection; it is an ever-developing conceptual residue of the constant stream of often difficult, actual moral judgments made by individuals and communities in response to the concrete ethical challenges which confront them. James pits himself stubbornly against any attempt to reduce this complex actual process to theorizing; he resists any attempt, as I have indicated previously, to 'substitute the content of ... [philosophers'] clean-shaven systems for that exuberant mass of goods with which all human nature is in travail, and groaning to bring to the light of day.'[26]

If it is true, then, as is often said to be the case, that James is utilitarian in certain aspects of his ethical thought, it must be added that he is no more willing to accept utilitarian abstractions 'made up in advance' than he is to accept any other abstractions made in advance. At bottom, the moral life is first and foremost a participation of some form, willing or unwilling, conventional or unconventional, thoughtful or superficial, in an ongoing historical process. This process

is nothing but the story of men's struggles from generation to generation to find the more and more inclusive order. *Invent some manner* of realizing your own ideals which will also satisfy the alien demands – that and that only is the path of peace! Following this path, society has shaken itself into one sort of relative equilibrium after another by a series of social discoveries quite analogous

to those of science. Polyandry and polygamy and slavery, private
warfare and liberty to kill, judicial torture and arbitrary royal
power have slowly succumbed to actually aroused complaints.[27]

At the heart of this process, then, which is the font of moral
life and moral understanding, there is a dialectical relation
between the irrepressible impulse, arising in the hearts of living
individuals and communities, to protest against being
demeaned and excluded, on the one hand, and, on the other, the
abstract moral *status quo* of the community. While the foregoing
protests challenge the *status quo*, the *status quo* is nevertheless
deserving of *prima facie* respect because it may well embody culturally the successful struggles of previous generations against
other forms of exclusion and degradation. The protests against
the *status quo*, however, for their part, are equally entitled to
*prima facie* benefit of the doubt, for they may well signal ways in
which the community's present moral abstractions covertly
sanction continuing forms of oppression.

Both the *status quo* and the 'actually aroused complaints'
against it, then, play central roles in the unfolding of the moral
understanding and behaviour of individuals and communities.
Neither is inviolable. The demands of aggrieved individuals
and communities must occasion constant reassessment of the
theoretical *status quo*, and vice versa. The resulting tension constitutes an unending historical aspiration after moral discernment, the results of which are only ever fragmentarily and
incompletely reflected in moral theory.

The core of James's account of the moral life, then, is neither
theory nor concrete demand, but a dialectic between the two
which is perpetually unfolding historically. Moral understanding arises out of participation in, and reflection upon, the

struggle and ... squeeze; and everlastingly the problem of how to
make them less. The anarchists, nihilists, and free-lovers; the free-
silverites, socialists, and single-tax men; the free-traders and civil-
service reformers; the prohibitionists and anti-vivisectionists; the
radical darwinians with their idea of the suppression of the weak,
– these and all the considerable sentiments of society arrayed

against them, are simply deciding through actual experiment by what sort of conduct the maximum amount of good can be gained and kept in the world. These experiments are to be judged, not *à priori*, but by actually finding, after the fact of their making, how much more outcry or how much appeasement comes about. What closet-solutions can possibly anticipate the result of trials made on such a scale? Or what can any superficial theorist's judgment be worth, in a world where every one of hundreds of ideas has its special champion already provided in the shape of some genius expressly born to feel it, and to fight to death on its behalf? The pure philosopher can only follow the windings of the spectacle, confident that the line of least resistance will always be towards the richer and the more inclusive arrangement, and that by one tack after another some approach to the kingdom of heaven is incessantly made.[28]

A willing and creative participation in the foregoing process acquires a certain distinctive character when participation is seen as being undertaken in collaboration with the divine. It is only in these terms of reference that the strenuous mood can be properly understood. The presence of such religious conviction does not change the basic nature of the moral life, however. It does not provide distinctive moral precepts of purportedly divine origin. The strenuous mood, rather, is an amplification of elements which already constitute the moral life. It is not a particular *state*, worthy of being pursued self-interestedly for its affective pleasures. Rather, it is, as I have said, a distinctive *character* which the divestment of self-interest acquires when the moral life involves religious terms of reference.

It is important to underscore in this connection the central place assigned by James to the active pursuit of moral *discernment*, rather than behaviour, in his account of the moral life. It is the character which the pursuit of discernment acquires, when undertaken within religious terms of reference, which lies at the heart of the strenuous mood. Given the thicket of conflicting interpretations of James's epistemology, we ought to proceed carefully in seeking to understand the nature of such discernment, and would be well served in this connection by taking our initial conceptual bearings from Iris Murdoch. There are striking similarities between the positions of Murdoch and James, and we can benefit a good deal from Murdoch's efforts, almost a century after James.

The inner life of the person in much recent philosophy, Murdoch observes, has come increasingly to be understood as constituted principally by the possession of language. Because language is a public phenomenon, its acquisition by the individual is essentially the acquisition of a constellation of publically shared meanings and conventions. Since the interiority of the individual is seen as being so extensively constituted by meanings and conventions, it too has come increasingly to be construed, therefore, as public in character. The view of the person which emerges in such an account is not the atomistic individual of Hume, for example, but is the individual's awareness of an impersonal complex of logical conventions. Such inner life is 'hazy, largely absent, and anyway "not part of the mechanism,"' which acts.[29] It is 'a shadow of life in public.'[30]

Not surprisingly, the search for a distinctive centre of personhood and the moral life under such conceptual conditions has sometimes shifted away from the publically-constituted life of reason, and towards volition. The self which emerges here, however, turns out to have been whittled down to fleeting, empty acts of choice. Behaviour seems to be little more than a 'sudden jumping of the isolated will in and out of an impersonal logical complex.'[31] In such a view, 'the agent, thin as a needle, appears in the quick flash of the choosing will.'[32] Given such a view of volition, 'there is no point of talking of "moral seeing" since there is nothing *morally* to see ... There is only the ordinary world which is seen with ordinary vision, and there is the will that moves within it.'[33] In sum, then, Murdoch finds that in much recent thought 'the idea of the agent as a privileged centre of will ... is retained, but, since the old-fashioned "self" no longer clothes him he appears as an isolated will operating with the concepts of "ordinary language," so far as the field of morals is concerned.[34]

While appreciative of the many important insights deriving in recent decades from a better philosophical understanding of language and its acquisition, Murdoch protests that the foregoing picture is deeply flawed. It fails, as James would also say, to grasp two major points of great significance. The first of these has to do with the relation between conception and action. I will return to this soon. The second has to do with the inherently *idiosyncratic* nature of language-acquisition and, therefore, the idiosyncratic character of reason itself. However public and shared the conventions of langauge may be, human beings assimilate language *historically* in such a way that each personality and life-story inevitably leaves a peculiar stamp on meanings. Language, in other words, however public the conventions are which constitute it, acquires subtle nuances of meaning which are peculiar to the individual. Such nuances differ not only from individual to individual, but also, over time, even within the life of each individual as well. 'We have a different image of courage at forty from that which we had at twenty,' Murdoch reminds us; 'a deepening process ... takes place.'[35]

There is no reason, moreover, to confine such deepening to weighty matters only. Differences of intellectual depth and insight occur in all areas of conceptualization. The painter, after years of thoughtful experiment with pigment, will have a much richer appreciation of something as simple as 'red' than will her artistically inexperienced neighbour.[36] At bottom, then, having appropriated a concept from what is admittedly the public domain, there is a significant degree to which one 'takes it away into his privacy.'[37]

As a consequence of the foregoing contextual character of language acquisition, there is a certain irreducible idiosyncrasy which unavoidably accrues to the life of reason. Such idiosyncrasy limits the extent to which the processes of reasoning, and the experience of 'reasonableness,' may be anticipated to be completely public and shared. 'Reasons are not necessarily and *qua* reasons public,' as Murdoch put it. 'They may be reasons for a very few, and none the worse for that. "I can't explain. You'd have to know her."'[38]

James is often driving at much the same point, I would argue, in his understanding and defence of the *reasonableness* which I have shown previously in this book to be a central property of propositions which are 'live,' even propositions which are live for only certain individuals. What we find in the actual conduct of the life of reason, James argues repeatedly, is an idiosyncratic depth and perspective which enter inevitably into all comprehension, reasoning, argument and belief. Such depth and perspective are indebted to a host of influences.

Not the least of such influences are the human being's 'simpler functions.' In deeply empirical cultures, however, 'the peculiar sources of joy connected with our simpler functions often dry up, and we grow stone-blind and insensible to life's more elementary and general goods and joys.'[39] James invites us to turn periodically from philosophy and theorizing to literature, therefore, in order to remind ourselves of this. Good literature far outpaces theory in its capacity to capture the subtleties and idiosyncracies of *actual* reasoning and argument. Drawing upon Robert Louis Stevenson, De Sénancour, Wordsworth, Whitman, Shelley, Tolstoy, and others, he amplifies the individual character of even the most mundane experiences, and the ways in which such individuality influences reasoning. The world is at one and the same time a place in which Wordsworth finds himself enthralled even by something as simple as the gravel on the highway,[40] and a place in which Schopenhauer finds 'the same recurrent inanities, the same dog barking, the same fly buzzing, forevermore.'[41] As James observes, 'of the kind of fibre of which such inanities consist is the material woven of all the excitements, joys, *and meanings* that ever were, or ever shall be, in this world' (emphasis added).[42]

Intellectual life, in its actual occurrence, then, is not just a seeing *that*. It is also a recognition of significance, meaning, depth, and much more, all of which is involved in the acquisition of moral understanding. Comprehension is often more a matter of *insight* than it is the acquisition of further information. There are close connections between this point and the centrality of insight and metaphor in James's epistemology. Norms for the responsible use of reason cannot ignore the notion of insight, the propensity of human beings to stumble repeatedly into a 'higher vision of an inner significance in what, until then, we had realized only in the dead external way.'[43] Such occurrences are often sudden and unexpected; they set before us 'a depth ... that constrains us to ascribe more reality to them than to all other experiences.'[44] They are also unpredictable, as likely to be found in an 'insolvent tramp or loafer'[45] as among the educated and sophisticated who made up the audience listening to James talking about a certain blindness in human beings.

The idiosyncratic and unpredictable character of rationality, so construed, will be resisted by many philosophers, Murdoch and James both anticipate, who seek to expunge such elements from epistemology in order to smooth the way for movement towards an ever greater domination of epistemology by empirical consensus and theory. Murdoch and James are right, however, to challenge cultural resistance to the idiosyncratic and contextual character of experience and langauge acquisition; they are right also to resist an understanding of the nature of reasonableness which ignores such formidable aspects of the actual conduct of reason in day-to-day life. This narrowing of the notion of reason precludes even the possibility of recognizing that 'there is ... something in the serious attempt to look compassionately at human things which automatically suggests that "there is more than this." The "there is more than this," if it is not to be corrupted by some sort of quasi-theological finality, must remain a very tiny spark of insight, something with, as it were, a metaphysical position but no metaphysical form. But it seems to me that the spark is real, and that great art is evidence of its reality.'[46]

The pursuit of moral discernment, for Murdoch, involves gradual movement, potentially at least, in this direction, and in the direction of recognizing a 'good' which, while indefinable in virtue its involvement in 'the infinite elusive character of reality,'[47] is nevertheless accessible to reason.

> I would suggest that at the level of serious common sense and of an ordinary non-philosophical reflection about the nature of morals it is perfectly obvious that goodness *is* connected with knowledge: not with impersonal, quasi-scientific knowledge of the ordinary world, whatever that may be, but with a refined and honest perception of what is really the case, a patient and just dis-

cernment and exploration of what confronts one, which is the result not simply of opening one's eyes but of a certain perfectly familiar kind of moral discipline.[48]

For James, such discernment also plays a central role in the moral life, and the strenuous mood is directly implicated in this. The strenuous mood has to do with the energy and commitment with which one pursues insight. This pursuit, moreover, is a matter of volition. One can *choose* whether or not to pursue 'patient and just discernment.' One can choose how to attend. Choices are constantly made to seek for what is titillatingly scurrilous, cheap, or spectacular, or for what is enduring and unassuming. Choices are made constantly to attend with empathy, or with the eyes of what Murdoch aptly refers to as the Freudian 'fat relentless ego.'

It is here, in the *work of attending*, that the activity of volition is above all to be found, for both Murdoch and James, and so the exercise of freedom 'cannot ... be separated from the idea of knowledge.'[49] The exercise of volition is 'a small piecemeal business which goes on all the time and not a grandiose leaping about unimpeded at important moments. The moral life, on this view, is something that goes on continually, not something that is switched off in between the occurrence of explicit moral choices. What happens in between such choices is indeed what is crucial.'[50]

Observe, Murdoch urges, 'what the work of attention is like, how continuously it goes on.'[51] Observe also 'how imperceptibly it builds up structures of value round about us,'[52] creating thereby the conceptual infrastructure for choices yet to be made. What is chosen in innumerable mundane instances is how to *see*, and it is in countless minute efforts that the die is cast for later so-called 'major' decisions in life. 'At crucial moments of choice most of the business of choosing is already over.'[53]

It is only when the foregoing relation of intellectual and volitional is in place that James and Murdoch are willing to consider action. Volition has centrally to do with building up ways of *seeing*; action takes care of itself. 'If we picture the agent as compelled by obedience to the reality he can see, he will not be saying "This is right," i.e., "I choose to do this," he will be saying "This is A B C D" ... and action will follow naturally.'[54]

That 'action will follow naturally' from such seeing is exactly what James also holds. For James, such a link is entirely understandable if we appreciate fully that 'consciousness is *in its very nature impulsive*.'[55] That is to say, 'all ideas have relations with some ... [motor] paths.'[56] It is not at the level of action that the work of volition should primarily be sought, then, but in the acquisition of *awareness* of a certain sort. The real core of the moral life, in such a view, and therefore of the strenuous mood as well, is the production of such awareness. Volition has to do with '*a relation between the mind and its "ideas*."' Action will take care of itself, for in the normal personality 'it is of the essence of all consciousness (or of the neural process which underlies it) to instigate movement of some sort.'[57]

James knew that such a proposal about the relation among intellect, volition and action would be controversial, and he defended it effectively and at length. The direct link between thought and action, he notes, is particularly evident in human 'ideo-motor' actions such as applying the brakes of a car or tying a common knot. The idea of doing such things will be found to flow without interruption into their execution. In all such actions, 'a movement *unhesitatingly and immediately* follows upon the idea of it.'

Simple motor activities, however, constitute only part of the life of activity. There are many ideas, he readily concedes, which we would expect to lead to action, but which seem not to do so. The conception by the alcoholic of his possible sobriety, for example, usually has little or no impact on his behaviour. Certain personalities entertain a host of ideas which never see the light of day in action. Abstract and unusual ideas, by comparison with more concrete and familiar ones, appear by and large to be powerless to move most people. The biblical notions, for example, that one ought to 'give to *all* who ask' and expect no return, or that one ought to turn the other cheek to the enemy, do not exactly spring forth in action on any significant scale even among those people who claim to embrace such principles.

Does this not suggest that only some conceptions are related directly to action, and that the difference between these and other conceptions is the intervention of will? The foregoing apparent exceptions, James argues, will not constitute exceptions to the close linking of consciousness and action if we appreciate that action has to do not simply with the *presence* of a conception to consciousness, but with the '*urgency ... with which ...* [an idea] *is able to compel attention and dominate in consciousness.*'[58]

Urgency has in part to do with the 'field' character of consciousness, as well as with affectivity. The intensity of a conception's presence to consciousness, that is, will vary, depending upon the relations among ideas sharing the conceptual field. The capacity of any one idea to move an agent, in other words, is deeply effected by its relationship with other ideas, and the affective state to which such alliances give rise. Conflicting ideas obstruct one anothers' natural tendency to issue in act. '*Every representation of a movement awakens in some degree the actual movement which is its object; and awakens it in a maximum degree whenever it is not kept from so doing by an antagonistic representation present simultaneously to the mind.*'[59] The point is directly relevant in the case of religion.

> One thing that ideas do is to contradict other ideas and keep us from believing them. An idea that thus negates a first idea may itself in turn be negated by a third idea, and the first idea may thus regain its natural influence over our belief *and determine our behaviour.* Our philosophical and religious development proceeds thus by credulities, negations and the negating of negations ... In general, whether a given idea shall be a live idea depends more on the person into whose mind it is injected than on the idea itself.[60]

Conflict among conceptions may inhibit acting on an idea for seconds, years or a lifetime, even though the inhibition may not be recognized as such. Careful reflection, however, reveals the presence of unnoticed inhibitory relationships among conceptions. In the process of reflection on some competing ideas during deliberation, for example, certain considerations can be found moving prominently to the foreground of consciousness. Behind these, however, there are others exerting their influence as well. If I am wrestling with myself about whether to keep a certain sum of money, so as to enlarge my business and grow wealthier, or whether to give that money to people in need, certain considerations come into prominence at one time, only to yield that place of prominence at another. At one point, for instance, I may be particularly struck by the arduousness of the labour by which I have come into possession of the money in question. At another point, however, I may experience an equally acute awareness of the suffering of those in need.

Such shifting foci constitute the foreground of an ever-changing deliberative scene. If deliberation were to consist only of this foreground it would be short-lived, and life would be extremely impulsive. This is in fact often the case with young children who require, on that account, the intervention of adults who can provide the relevant background restraints. It is the background of deliberation that affects the urgency with which particular convictions register at the moment. Such background synoptic awareness 'tells us that all this [in the foreground of deliberation] is provisional; that the weakened reasons will wax strong again, and the stronger weaken.'[61]

This complex interplay of intellectual influences can easily obscure the direct link between awareness and action that James wants to establish because it makes it seem as though only some conceptions lead to action, while others do not. In fact, however, it is the *relationship among* conceptions which accounts for the apparent differences among the capacities of some conceptions rather than others to arouse action. Decisions which resolve competition among conceptions take many different forms. All of them, however, in James's reckoning, involve in one way or another releasing a conception from constraint by conflicting conceptions.

On some occasions, for example, the sifting of competing ideas gradually yields a satisfying intellectual resolution on behalf of one particular conception. On other occasions, resolution may take the form of subsuming an intellectual conflict under a broader general heading which provides the basis for resolution. I may previously have learned from my business experience, for example, that virtually all courses of action which require an overextension of funds in a company the size of mine create serious problems in the long run. Therefore, I have adopted the general rule that it is better on the whole to take fiscally conservative decisions. I subsume the particular, intractable choice with which I am currently struggling, under the general heading of that rule. Faced with a situation in which additional property has become available adjacent to my own, into which my business could potentially expand, my otherwise inconclusive deliberations can be resolved by classifying the competing options within a broader fame of reference. On this basis, the idea that I should refrain from acting on the opportunity gains a decisive upper hand. Action, under such circumstances, is the result of *re-envisioning* the particular situation before me. '*In action as in reasoning, then, the great thing is the quest of the right conception.*'[62]

Is it not the case, however, that some instances of deliberation do not yield clear-cut victories of one conception over others? James concedes that there are many such cases. Sometimes there does not seem to be anything available to swing the balance decisively in one direction or another. Deliberation may grow wearisome under the burden of indecision, and a certain urgency to resolve matters may emerge, but without any accompanying clarity. Such situations resolve themselves in different ways. Sometimes a fortuitous event occurs which tips the balance in favour of one option. An unexpected and unusually robust economic upturn, for example, may be enough to swing the balance in favour of one view in a business matter. In other cases, we simply allow ourselves to drift to one position or another because the outcome of neither alternative is seen as particularly significant in the long run. There are yet other cases in which a great upheaval of perspective in the personality as a whole – a 'change of heart' – may shift the entire intellectual scene, including particular matters under deliberation. A deep personal impact precipitated by the unexpected death of a beloved friend, for example, may so alter my view about wealth in general that the question of whether or not to expand my business is no longer even an issue.

At bottom, however, no matter how varied the circumstances,

James argues, the basic link between conception and action constantly reveals itself to careful scrutiny, as does the intertwining of volition, affectivity, and the fluidity of conception. This intertwining can be seen particularly clearly, for example, in instances involving attempts to protect present conceptions.

> The cooling advice which we get from others when the fever-fit is on us is the most jarring and exasperating thing in life. Reply we cannot, so we get angry; for by a sort of self-preserving instinct which our passion has, it feels that these chill objects, if they once but gain a lodgment, will work and work until they have frozen the very vital spark from out of all our mood ... *if they can once get a quiet hearing.*[63]

Attention, if it is directed even to the small dissenting voice until that voice receives a hearing, then, 'begins to call up its own congerers and associates and ends by changing the disposition of the man's consciousness altogether. And with his consciousness his action changes, for the new object, once stably in possession of the field of his thoughts, infallibly produces its own motor effects. The difficulty lies in the gaining possession of that field.'[64] It is this 'strain of the attention' which is the basic act of will.[65] *'The essential achievement of the will, in short, when it is most "voluntary," is to attend to a difficult object and hold it fast before the mind.* The so-doing *is* the *fiat*; and it is a mere physiological incident that when the object is thus attended to, immediate motor consequences should ensue. *Effort of attention is thus the essential phenomenon of will.'*[66]

The pivotal contention here, then, is that 'we ought to look for the secret of an idea's impulsiveness, not in any peculiar relations which it may have with paths of motor discharge, – for *all* ideas have relations with some such paths, – but rather in a preliminary phenomenon, the *urgency, namely, with which it is able to compel attention and dominate in consciousness'.*[67] In sum, from the point of view of ethics, *'to sustain a representation, to think,* is in short, the only moral act.'[68]

Having emphasized in the foregoing pages the link between volition and conception, and the fluidity and idiosyncrasy of conception, I risk inadvertently strengthening the subjectivistic stereotypes of James which this book is devoted to overturning. Does not such a portrayal lead precisely to the wishful thinking with which he has been charged throughout this century? If the many observations I have made throughout this book about the circumscription of subjectivity do not allay such concerns immediately, perhaps a few further observations specifically about James's understanding of the moral life will help.

Far from reducing 'the good' to personal utility and commending wishful thinking, James's position promotes an objectivist account of the good, and a strident repudiation of self-interest, notwithstanding the fluidity of conceptualization, and the profound influence on thought by volition. His emphasis on the contingently historical and epistemologically idiosyncratic nature of rationality and moral discernment aims at impeding the domination of ethics by theory, not at relativizing ethics. The domination by theory, he insists repeatedly, too easily allows people to escape from the recalcitrant pressures of actual day to day life, and such pressures are indispensable guides in seeking objectivity in ethics. Excessive abstraction allows the theorist to escape from entanglement in the 'exuberant mass of goods' which compete in day-to-day life. It allows for retreat into the serene, less troubling world of thin 'clean shaven systems,' and for escape from the difficult lessons and challenges of the *particulars* of life which are central to Radical Empiricism.

Such escape, however, is the root of wishful thinking and subjectivism, for James. It is only when the idiosyncratic and historical elements of actual, concrete experience are allowed to have their full impact on reflection that we can achieve 'any perception of life's meaning on a large *objective* scale' (emphasis added).[69] It is only *concrete* experience, in all its contingent and idiosyncratic richness, which will curb the propensity to theorize self-interestedly. An amplification of the idiosyncratic elements of moral insight, in James's account, then, has nothing to do with a promotion on his part of the 'wayward personal standards'[70] which critics are fond of imputing to pragmatists. On the contrary, 'we hold to it,' James says clearly, 'that there is a truth to be ascertained'[71] in the moral domain, a truth which demands the relinquishment of wayward personal standards. 'Our environment encourages us not to be philosophers but partisans. The philosopher, however, cannot, so long as he clings to his own ideal of objectivity, rule out any ideal from being heard. He is confident, and rightly confident, that the simple taking counsel of his own intuitive preferences would be certain to end in a mutilation of the fullness of the truth.'[72]

The adoption of wayward personal standards, in disregard for the lessons of the historical and concrete domain, James warns, will be met with a destructive backlash *by the world itself.* The natural order will most certainly recoil, he says, against the intrusion of unbridled self-interest in belief and behaviour; 'the good which we have wounded returns to plague us with interminable crops of consequential damages, compunctions and regrets.'[73]

The idiosyncratic element of James's position, then, must not be interpreted relativistically. The idiosyncratic fragmentariness of any one individual's moral vision is not by any means the last word either for her or her community; it is only part of a larger picture which transcends such perspectival limitations, and which James is eager to protect.

> Hands off: neither the whole of truth nor the whole of good is revealed to any single observer, although each observer gains a partial superiority of insight from the peculiar position in which he stands. Even prisons and sick-rooms have their special revelations. It is enough to ask of each of us that he should be faithful to his own opportunities and make the most of his own blessings, without presuming to regulate the rest of the vast field.[74]

The consultation of idiosyncratic 'special revelations' is an indispensable part of seeking 'the whole truth,' and of aspiring to a 'genuine and real foothold'[75] in the pursuit of sound moral discernment. It is part of the process of developing a *system of truth*[76] in ethics which may 'settle the true order of human obligations,'[77] albeit in a way which will never be entirely finished, nor separable from the ongoing consultation of the unfolding historical order.

If the moral life, for James, is first and foremost about attending, and about the pursuit of moral discernment, then the strenuous mood must be thought of in terms of a certain character which such attending and pursuit come to possess under the influence of religious conviction. When augmented religiously, the moral life involves a particularly 'strenuous' and adventurous search for sound moral vision. The strenuous mood is an elevation of the fervour with which the pursuit of moral discernment is undertaken, and it is a heightening of the willing, vigilant participation in the historical dialectic of theory and demand which this involves. Such effort cannot be separated from imagination and affectivity. It is not the 'thin' seeing of theory, but a 'thick' seeing involving empathy, character, courage, and much else.

It is with this fuller account of the strenuous mood than one normally finds that we should return to the familiar interpretations and criticisms of James described at the beginning of this chapter which charge him with having sponsored wishful thinking and with having confused belief and hypothesis-adoption. To what extent are these interpretations and criticisms congruent with the depiction of the strenuous mood developed so far in this chapter? Is it plausible to take James as having proposed a movement beyond evidence based solely on prudential considerations geared to the acquisition of the purportedly desirable consequences of theism, and which fault him for having commended a movement ahead of evidence on the basis of an inadequate appreciation of the differences between belief and hypothesis-adoption?

The most recent version of the first of these positions – the prudential reading of James – has been provided by James Wernham. Wernham's version is a particularly rigorous one, for it denies even hypothetical viability to theism, thereby making the motive of adopting theism entirely prudential. His version also stands apart in its recognition of the central place of the strenuous mood in James's philosophy of religion.

According to Wernham, we cannot now decide the relative merits of theism or atheism on evidential grounds. The responsible course of conduct intellectually, therefore, would be to suspend belief and treat theism as a hypothetical possibility. The problem here, however, in Wernham's account, is that even a hypothetical theism does not hold much promise. That is to say, if a hypothetical theism were going to contribute to the advance of inquiry, in Wernham's judgment, there would have to be some means of discovering whether the states of affairs which theism would anticipate do in fact turn out to be the case. At present, we know nothing of the ultimate destiny of the world, about which theism has much to say, and on which a hypothetical theism's vindication would be significantly dependent. We also know nothing about the ultimate verdict of those who, in the course of human history, will turn out to have been willing to give theism the benefit of the doubt in anticipation of possible future revelations of its merits and liabilities. As a 'tool of inquiry,'[78] then, hypothetical theism has overwhelming liabilities, in Wernham's assessment.

However, the luxury of suspending belief and abandoning hope of verifying an hypothesis is not always accompanied by the luxury of being able to delay action as well, and this is the case with theism, according to Wernham. As Pascal puts it, we are embarked upon the affair of life; we have no choice about whether or not to choose how to live it. In Wernham's view, it is within our power to choose to live as theists, atheists or agnostics, even while suspending judgment on the foregoing intellectual matters. Whichever way one's choice goes, Wernham argues, it will be a 'pure gamble' which has nothing to do with evidence. He who chooses theism is like the mountain climber in *The Will to Believe* who, Wernham holds, has 'no ground for believing' that the jump across the crevice can be made successfully. Neither is there 'ground ... for believing that he cannot'[79] successfully make the leap. Here, as in many other examples offered by Wernham, the gamble is a wholly personal undertaking; passional nature is on its own.

Why would one make such a gamble on theism? What would favour a decision for theism in the absence of sufficient evidence on behalf of either alternative in the theistic gamble? It is prudential considerations alone which favour this decision, in Wernham's account. Unlike other commentators, Wernham should be commended for having recognized the important place of the strenuous mood in this connection. It would be foolish not to choose theism because an '"immediate reward" ... attaches to the act itself of betting on that side. That reward James called "the strenuous mood".'[80] A life lived in the strenuous mood is 'the best life whether or not it was also the right life.'[81] It would be imprudent to pass up the chance of enjoying the personal benefits of the strenuous mood, Wernham says, and the acquisition of that state justifies taking the gamble on theism.

The motive for adopting theism, then, on Wernham's account of James, is a wholly personal one: the desire to secure its immediate subjective benefits. The choice for theism, even if theism turns out to be factually false, will occasion the benefit of that desirable state. If theism turns out to be true, the prospects are even better; much more will be added to the improvement of this present life, a life which will already have benefited by having been lived in the strenuous mood. One is 'forced' on prudential grounds, therefore, Wernham argues, not epistemological or ethical ones, to opt for theism.

What exactly is the 'immediate reward' of betting on theism? Unfortunately, Wernham, like other commentators on James, never really gets around to exploring the nature of the strenuous mood sufficiently to clarify this matter, and this failure completely undermines his, and other prudential accounts of James. I hope it is clear by now, given the observations of Chapter One and of the present chapter, that the strenuous mood is not the unambiguously desirable state which Wernham and others assume it to be. It is the easy-going mood, not the strenuous mood, James was seen in 'The Moral Philosopher and the Moral Life' to have pointed out, which avoids ill. The strenuous mood, by contrast, invites many forms of substantial but eminently avoidable ills. It leads, in the pursuit of moral discernment, to 'agonizing ourselves'[82] over many matters such as the contribution we can make to future generations, for example, and to wrestling, in a way which sometimes involves painful dissent from one's community, with a myriad of other moral matters. It calls for a moral heroism and self-denial, the personal price of which is not at all well represented by the cheerier description of the strenuous mood as occasioning 'the keenest possibilities of zest'[83] in human life. Such zest it may occasion, but at a personal cost from which any sensible person ought initially, at least, to shrink; a cost which has been universally overlooked in the literature on James's thought. The strenuous mood actually *invites* many ills which one is able to endure 'if only the greater ideal be attained.'[84] Its intellectual demands are arduous, for the strenuous mood is very much the enemy of comforting theoretical solutions to difficult intellectual questions, satisfying declarations of comprehensiveness of understanding, and gratifying resolutions of perplexing tensions among competing conceptions.

The often trying features of the strenuous mood bear little resemblance to the better-known soothing consequences attributed to theism by Freud, for example, and assumed by most commentators on James. Prudential readings of James, however, seem on the whole to be much more congruent with the Freudian version of theism than they are with James's. The Freudian theism of *The Future of an Illusion*, for instance, generates the consoling security of confidently believing oneself to be protected by an almighty Father, and to be the eventual recipient of future rewards for present forbearance and religious conformity.

James, by striking contrast, vigorously attacks conventional moral conformism as often deeply at odds with real moral integrity. Such conformism frequently amounts to little more than the bland 'moral holiday' from the ascetical and creative pursuit of moral discernment and real justice, a holiday which seems so predictably to accompany conventional religious belief in an omnipotent and apocalyptic divine Solver-of-all-human-problems. Such a moral holiday differs greatly from the struggle for moral discernment and insight described earlier in this chapter, and from the concrete, indispensable collaboration with the divine described in Chapter 1.

The strenuous mood leads not to a secure, conformist moral holiday but away from it. Rather than Freud's comfortable believer, one would do better to choose as a representative of the Jamesean strenuous mood someone like Hans Jäggerstätter.[85] Jäggerstätter, an Austrian peasant accustomed to fighting in his younger days, was beheaded by German authorities on 9 August 1943 for refusing to fight in the German military during World War II. James would have seen in Jäggerstätter, I think, an exemplification of the strenuous mood not just because of Jäggerstätter's resistance to the Nazis, or because of his invocation of a religious basis for his principles. James would have seen him as exemplifying the strenuous mood, rather, because of his resistance also to the considerable efforts of his church pastor, and of his bishop and townsfolk, all of whom encouraged him to participate in the war, if only to kill Bolsheviks. James would have commended in Jäggerstätter the recognition, in painful, and ultimately fatal defiance of convention, of the ways in which his countrymen and church, as well as the Nazis, had failed to see the centrality of inclusiveness in the moral life – an inclusiveness which includes Bolsheviks – and the unusual demands which such inclusiveness may make upon the individual under particular historical conditions.

It is Jäggerstätter, not the bland Freudian believer, who best embodies the insightful, inventive and often ascetical and self-sacrificing vigour of the strenuous mood in its allegiance to the fundamentally inclusive character of the moral life. That mood bears little resemblance to the pedestrian utilitarianism so often imputed to James's ethics, or to the safe haven of Freudian theism. One 'reward,' to use Wernham's term, therefore, which attached itself to Jäggerstätter's strenuous mood was the loss of his head, something which prudential accounts of James would likely have difficulty accommodating.

The intellectual and theological challenges of the strenuous mood are as unsettling as its ascetical demands. Genuine religiosity, as James understands it, does not provide intellectual or dogmatic peace. As I indicated near the beginning of this chapter, James says that religion sets the mundane historical order in the context of a broader, supernatural order. In so doing, it creates an 'infinite perspective,' and thereby gives to the intellectual field a horizon of 'infinitude and mystery.'[86] This horizon of infinitude and mystery, however, could be reasonably anticipated to have an unsettling, not a stabilizing and comforting effect on intellectual life as a whole. It would undermine, not encourage, certitude about the details of theological as well as secular matters, and would heighten attentiveness to the possibility of unanticipated ways of thinking and understanding. In *The Will to Believe*, James vigorously rejects the notion that 'religion primarily seeks to solve the intellectual mystery of the world.'[87] What religion does is sustain a tension between the mundane historical fact of existence, and the horizon of infinitude and mystery against which that fact is viewed. It thereby sustains difficult *questions*, and it is such questions, not dogmatic formulae, which are the life-blood of real religiosity, for James.

> However particular questions connected with our individual destinies may be answered, it is only by acknowledging them as genuine questions, and living in the sphere of thought which they open up, that we become profound. But to live thus is to be religious ... By being religious we establish ourselves in possession of ultimate reality at the only points at which reality is given us to guard [our own concrete existence].[88]

In the 'half-wild, half-saved universe' envisioned by religion there is no telling what may turn out to be the case, and such uncertainty loosens the hold of conventional thought and undermines claims to certainty in all domains, along with the intellectual security which attends these. In place of certitude, the religious perspective would generate not comforting assuredness, but an alert attentiveness, a being-on-the-lookout which energetically probes beyond the conventional and the dogmatic, like James's intellectual heros such as Tolstoy, who developed an uncommonly insightful appreciation of the moral demands arising out of the proliferation of violence; Whitman, who saw a significance in parts of nature considered insignificant by his contemporaries; Louis Agassiz, who singled out features of the natural order which escaped the notice of his colleagues, and so on.

In the theological domain, an intellectual horizon broadened by the strenuous mood would be no less subversive of certainty and security than it is in secular matters. It would not furnish pat and personally consoling metaphysical theories or pseudo-scientific answers which close questions in the way, for example, that the Vatican tried theologically to close questions which Galileo rightly recognized not to admit of theological answers. Neither would it be exhausted by any body of dogmatic pronouncements, something from which *The Varieties of Religious Experience* is devoted in great part to freeing the experiential element of live theism. There is no doubt that religion is often pressed into the service of the desire to close questions, providing thereby a convenient and personally advantageous 'God-of-the-gaps,' as Dietrich Bonhoeffer put it.

Religion so construed, however, has no place in James's thought. In James's account, religion does not provide satisfying and consoling immutable dogmas to which one would be prudent to cling in order to be at peace. On the contrary, the tension that one finds in the strenuous mood between the basic orientation to a transcendent and the need to specify, via indispensable overbeliefs, the nature of that transcendent, would be a source of much intellectual perplexity and uncertainty which is unknown to the easy-going mood, or to the Freudian believer. This tension is an inescapable corollary, it seems to me, of James's account of the strenuous mood, for the fundamental orientation to the transcendent which characterizes religiosity at its root, in James's account, is an orientation which is always historical in its actual occurrence, and so takes place within the terms of reference of a variety of specific conceptual systems. Not all, or even any one such system can do justice to the reality which they aspire to describe.

James, therefore, rightly holds the conceptual aspect of religiosity in a tension with its horizon of infinitude and mystery, a theme which pervades *The Varieties of Religious Experience*. Particular dogmatic beliefs constitute a necessary hypothetical[89] element of live theism, but must always be held only tentatively and uncomfortably in recognition of their potential insufficiency. The resulting tension between the ever-developing and often inadequate theoretical elements of theism, and the mysterious transcendent horizon of the intellectual life as a whole, lies at the heart of *The Varieties of Religious Experience* and occasions a range of intellectual perplexities and uncertainties which are far removed from the self-assured theological dogmatist or the Freudian believer.

Overall, then, the strenuous mood could be anticipated to create many perplexing questions, theological and otherwise. In this it is strikingly at variance with the comfort and self-assurance of the easy-going mood. Neither Wernham nor other commentators even include a consideration of such matters in their prudential accounts of James. While James did claim that the vigorous engagement of life characterizing the strenuous mood awakens a deeply rewarding 'zest,' the details that he provides about the form of life which generates this zest indicate that it comes at an uncomfortably high price, both ascetically and intellectually. This would likely be shunned, as it in fact has been generation after generation, even by many of those who claim to embrace religions subscribing to the inclusive counter-cultural love of enemy, identification with the outcast, and wariness of dogmatism.

The longstanding prudential views of James's association of theism with its purportedly pleasurable consequences uniformly ignore such important details about the strenuous mood, and are gravely compromised by that oversight. Many of the actual 'consequences' which James associated with the strenuous mood would scarcely motivate the adoption of the belief state, which supposedly leads to them. We should also recall once again in this connection that James explicitly rules out the possibility that consequences of *any* kind, pleasurable or otherwise, would make possible the creation of a new belief. The belief state cannot be brought into existence voluntarily by an individual, even if she clearly recognizes the beneficial consequences which would flow from possessing it, a point which James will be seen later to have appreciated in Pascal's position. No amount of personal desire for the subjective benefits of the strenuous mood can by itself create the intellectual horizon from which those subjective benefits flow, and upon which they are dependent, as will be seen in greater detail below.

If it is not prudential considerations which would legitimate belief in advance of evidence, perhaps James was arguing that the nature of inquiry itself requires this initiative. Russell and others have read James this way, but have contended that such a position involves a confusion of belief and hypothesis-adoption. I turn, therefore, to the second of the main lines of criticism levelled at James's philosophy of religion throughout this century. James, I will argue, was not at all unclear about the differences between belief and hypothesis-adoption, as further inquiry into the strenuous mood will bear out. He chose to defend belief rather than hypothesis-adoption in the case of theism for clear and sound reasons.

Wernham provides a helpful contemporary entrances into this issue. He rightly points out that there is a paradoxical need under some circumstances for human beings to run ahead of evidence in order to be evidentially responsible. He rightly asks 'whether "believe" is really the right word' to use in relation to the position advanced by James on this matter with respect to religion.[90] Are we dealing, in cases of religion, with movement ahead of evidence which should take the form of belief, hypothesis-adoption, or some other kind of response; an action of some kind, perhaps? 'If James's argument [in *The Will to Believe*] is to be one for believing theism, he will have to argue that the option posed by theism is forced, and momentous too, from the point of view of belief.'[91]

Wernham's judgment on this issue is that James 'gives no ... argument'[92] on behalf of a need to believe, nor should he have given one, for evidential considerations do not warrant belief, and it is not necessary to believe in order to inquire hypothetically into a certain intellectual possibility, or to act upon it. James failed to understand the need to distinguish between belief, hypothesis-adoption, and gambling; he 'did not choose between these different things: he chose all of them,'[93] and in so doing carelessly ignored important differences among them.

Certainly, Wernham is right to insist upon appropriate distinctions being made here. I may sometimes be forced to form hypotheses in advance of adequate evidence on their behalf, for example, but I am not forced to believe such hypotheses in advance of convincing evidence on their behalf. I may sometimes be forced as well to act in advance of adequate evidence, as when I come to a fork in a road, but may once again not be forced to believe anything regarding some aspects, at least, of the choices involved in such action. It would seem, then, that it may not have been belief but hypothesis-adoption, or perhaps action of some kind, that James was really talking about in his essay, but that he was unclear about the relation among these.

James, however, was clear on this matter. He was well aware of the differences between believing and unbelieving theisms and he deliberately chose to argue on behalf of the former. His comments about Pascal in *The Will to Believe* in particular reveal this awareness, although those comments have been poorly interpreted by Wernham, and ignored by almost everyone else. As even Wernham himself acknowledges, James argued that a 'faith "adopted wilfully after ... a mechanical calculation" can be a sham only, a counterfeit faith.'[94] James repeatedly asserts that religiosity, in its unbelieving mechanical form, is such a 'sham,' and that it is a form in which religiosity is 'put it its last trumps.'[95]

Pascal also thought ill of such a religiosity, James judges. Pascal was defending something which had 'far other springs'[96] than self-interest. It is only at the end of Pascal's argument that this becomes clear, however, a stage of the argument which Wernham would prefer that we ignore, for it links the state which in Pascal's argument is essentially the equivalent of James's strenuous mood, to belief alone.

Late in Pascal's wager argument an important development occurs. The sceptic discovers, to his surprise, that there is a crucial respect in which his prudential gamble, which is strikingly similar to Wernham's version of James, has not worked out as expected. Just when the wager argument seems to have carried the day, an unanticipated complication develops. The sceptic's aspiration after the theism which has been shown to be *personally* advantageous falls unexpectedly short. What he discovers is that a peculiar and unanticipated discontinuity exists between a hypothetical, wagered theism, based on the pursuit of personal advantage, and the form of theism characterizing actual religious believers. He discovers, moreover, that his own best efforts are of no avail in extending his present unbelieving theism to that further believing level.

The wager argument, in other words, has shown and convinced the sceptic that theism is personally important and beneficial. It is something, therefore, that prudence would direct him to embrace, as Wernham also holds. What the sceptic also discovers, however, to his consternation, is that he is unable to embrace it in the form in which it is embraced by actual religious people. Why should the skeptic care about this? Wernham argues stridently that he should not. There is 'nothing at all' for him to worry about in this respect; 'his problem is a non-problem.'[97] So pervasively influential in Wernham's case is a determination to drive apart hypothesis-adoption, belief, and wagering that he finds the sceptic's worry about being unable to connect the wager with belief to be a 'curious response.'[98] Faith and hypothesis-adoption are unrelated, Wernham insists over and over again, and so there is no reason to linger over the sceptic's concern that his mechanically adopted hypothetical theism cannot be extended into a believing theism. It does not matter. Wernham even tries exegetically to unhinge the sceptic's dismay about being unable to believe, from the wager argument which precedes it in Pascal's text. The issue of faith is raised only in the final stages of Pascal's wager argument, Wernham contends, and this stage is merely a 'sequel' which comes after 'the argument proper is now complete.'[99]

Wernham's efforts to the foregoing effect notwithstanding, Pascal's sceptic is plainly worried, and his worries are anything but an unrelated addendum to the wager argument; they are an explicit extension of the wager. Having been brought to recognize the merits of adopting theism, the sceptic only now becomes aware that there is yet another, unanticipated hurdle before him; he discovers that he is unable to lay hold of these merits. It is the gap between the hypothetical and believing theisms which comes to the fore here, because certain consequences attend one form of theism, but not the other. He is stuck recognizing the value of something that he cannot lay hold of, and it is only this which would make sense of the tone of dismay in his plea that 'I ... am so made that I cannot believe. What, then, would you have me do?'[100]

Such perplexity would make no sense whatever if it were cut

off, as Wernham tries to do, from the text and the mechanical theism which precede it, for perplexity is directly related to the achievements of reason which have led up to this point in Pascal's essay. The role of reason is clear: 'reason brings you to this,' the sceptic is told, it has shown the importance of believing, and the prudence of doing so. It has also, however, revealed an inability to believe.[101] The latter is as much a part of reason's contribution as the former, Pascal says, and together the two foregoing lessons constitute the contribution that reason is capable of making at this stage in the sceptic's life. It is not more 'increase in proofs' that is needed, counsels Pascal. Philosophical argument has done its job by successfully showing to the sceptic the merits of theism, and by showing him the road that lies still ahead, a road, however, along which reason has also shown the sceptic that it is unable by itself to lead him at the hypothetical level. A wager argument cannot bring into existence the form of theism whose personal merits it is capable of exhibiting. It cannot create a *live* theism. Even a clear recognition of the benefits of theism, in other words, cannot occasion the form of theism which will give rise to those benefits.

James recognized, with Pascal, the possibility of arguing as Wernham does, of holding that one should bet on theism with a view to one's self-interest, regardless of whether theism is true or not, because its beneficial consequences would justify such a bet. James also recognized that theism could be adopted hypothetically as well as in a believing form. He rejected these alternatives, however, and recognized that Pascal had done likewise. The theism in which Pascal was really interested had 'far other springs' than self-interest, as James observed. The only purpose involved in the 'mechanical' element of Pascal's wager argument – and, analogously, James's appeals to scientific 'hypothesis' vocabulary in *The Will to Believe* – is to provide a 'last desperate snatch at a weapon against the hardness of the unbelieving heart.'[102] Such appeals might at least unearth the remnants of an existing live theism in a cultural atmosphere ill-disposed to it.

As a first stage in responding to charges against James for having confused belief, hypothesis-adoption, and wagering, then, it can be said that James, like Pascal, was clearly aware that he had chosen to defend the belief state. He knew what he was doing. Both James and Pascal distinguish sharply between nonbelieving and believing theisms, and both do so because they deliberately associate the beneficial consequences of theism exclusively with the belief state.

The next stage in responding to charges that James confused belief and hypothesis-adoption involves a closer inquiry into why James would have adopted the position above. What is characteristic of analyses such as Wernham's and others as well, is the basic assumption that the state of belief, in the case of theism at any rate, does not essentially differ intellectually from hypothesis-adoption or some other form of moving ahead of available evidence when it comes to the strenuous mood. It is assumed that the belief state does not bring with it any distinctive consequences which would not be found in hypothesis-adoption or a gamble. Wernham, for example, sees no differences among belief, hypothesis-adoption, and gambling when it comes to theism. This is not to say, he admits, that believing and unbelieving theisms are completely indistinguishable. 'No doubt,' he concedes, 'some benefits attach to believing that God exists which do not attach to betting that he does.'[103] Wernham does not spell out what these might be, however, and there is no indication that, whatever they are, a believing theism would add anything to a hypothetical or a wagered theism in the pursuit of the intellectual and evidential merits of theism. It is just as well, therefore, in Wernham's account, that James neglected 'to argue that the option posed by theism is forced, and momentous too, from the point of view of belief,' because it is not.

On this point, Wernham's error is instructive. The option posed by theism is in fact forced from the point of view of belief, for James, because the strenuous mood is a function uniquely of belief. Wernham's misconstrual of James on this matter is partly exegetical. According to Wernham, James thought that 'the capacity for ... [the strenuous mood] could be activated ... by postulating theism, not just by believing it.'[104] In support of such a contention, James is cited to the effect that 'we, as would-be philosophers, must *postulate* a divine thinker, and pray for the victory of the religious cause ... so that our postulation of him after all serves only to let loose in us the strenuous mood' (emphasis added).[105] This statement certainly appears to associate the strenuous mood with a nonbelieving as well as with a believing theism, and appears moreover to support Wernham's argument.

While well-chosen, this single sentence from James is the entirety of the textual support provided by Wernham on behalf of an association of the strenuous mood with a nonbelieving, as well as a believing theism. This thinness of support on such a pivotal issue is not surprising, for the sentence cited turns out to be one of the loneliest in James's corpus, if it is taken literally. For one thing, it cuts against the grain of much in the very essay in which it is found, according to which the strenuous mood is said to occur 'when we *believe* that a God is there' (emphasis added);[106] it 'is set free in those who have religious *faith*' (emphasis added).[107] It also cuts dramatically against the grain of the entirety of the *Varieties of Religious Experience* which, from beginning to end, repeatedly asserts an association of the strenuous mood exclusively with religious belief. Religion, James says, 'wherever it is an active thing, involves *a belief* in ideal presences, and a belief that in our prayerful communion with them, work is done, and something real comes to pass' (emphasis added).[108] Moreover, between active belief and theoretical or hypothetical theisms there is a world of difference. 'He who lives the life of it [religion], however narrowly, is a better servant than he who merely knows about it, however much. Knowledge about life is one thing; effective occupation of a place in life, with its dynamic currents passing through your being, is another.'[109]

There are more than exegetical flaws in Wernham's analysis of James on the relation between belief and the strenuous mood, however. Wernham also fails to grasp the inseparability of the intellectual and personal elements of the strenuous mood, and the dependency of that mood on belief because of this inseparability. At the purely hypothetical or non-believing level, which Wernham himself strongly emphasizes involves no convictions whatever about the world, there would be no reason why theism should have any personal impact at all. What occasions the personal component of the strenuous mood is the connection which the individual makes between herself, as an existing person, and certain metaphysical beliefs. As a part of reality, that is, the individual is personally implicated in particular metaphysical contentions about reality as a whole. One makes this connection not just because of a personal desire or hope that it is so, or in order to attain personal edification, but because it is philosophically appropriate to do so.

Believed – live – theism, then, because it involves the conviction that certain metaphysical propositions are true, also involves a crucial connection between the individual, as a particular existent, and those propositions about existence in general. What is believed, what is held to be a fact about the world, implicates me insofar as I am a piece of that world, and certain affective responses to this connection are entirely appropriate, and are constitutive of the personal component of the strenuous mood. It is belief, in the case of theism, then, which causes the abstract theological contentions about the nature of the world to implicate the subject herself, to register with a personal 'pinch,' as James calls it; to be for the individual not just more abstractions which have no particular implications for one's existence, but part of what James calls a 'full fact,' – 'a conscious field *plus* its object as felt or thought of *plus* an attitude towards the object *plus* the sense of a self to whom the attitude belongs.'[110]

Even Russell conceded that the edifying consequences of theistic belief would be appropriate if theism were factually true. A believed theism uniquely involves the assertion of such factuality, and a recognition of the implications for the believer herself of the purported facts. Whether the believer is correct in asserting factuality of the propositions involved certainly has to be addressed, and I will return to this matter shortly. The point here, however, is that in instances of belief, the individual does assert such factuality, and it is upon the strength of this assertion that the full emergence of the personal component of the strenuous mood is contingent. The inseparability of the personal elements of the strenuous mood from intellectual assent links that mood with the belief state in a way which not only undermines criticisms of James for having confused belief and hypothesis-adoption, but also undermines prudential readings of *The Will to Believe* which see him as having advocated the formation of a belief in order to secure its desirable consequences, without regard for intellectual considerations.

The foregoing link between the belief state and the strenuous mood is further strengthened by another distinctive aspect of religious belief. In addition to the broadening of the general intellectual horizon about which I have already spoken above, a more specific intellectual element is to be found in many cases of live theism which James could be reasonably expected to have associated with the strenuous mood. James's extensive research involved in producing *The Varieties of Religious Experience* made it apparent to him, as many others have held,[111] that the religious experiences often accompanying live theism involve a distinctive noetic element which has evidential significance with respect to theism, as I indicated in Chapter One. The kind of theistic belief with which James is concerned is not the 'dull habit'[112] which carries many a purported believer numbly through her weekly rituals, but a theism possessing deep roots and experiential force. The noetic element of religious experience should not be confined to a handful of mystics. James warns his audience that *Varieties* includes a disproportionate number of unusual and mystical anecdotes for methodological reasons; an understanding of the normal is enhanced by an examination of its exaggerated forms. In its nonexaggerated form, James contends on a number of occasions, religious experience can be found empirically to be widespread among theists.

Live theism, then, as an actual phenomenon, often possesses certain distinctive noetic characteristics. Many experiences reported in *Varieties of Religious Experience* are, in this respect, 'as convincing to those who have them as any direct sensible experience can be.'[113] Such experiences are reported in terms not just of personal edification or subjective feeling, I emphasize, but in terms of 'genuine perceptions of truth.'[114] The phenomenon of 'perceiving truths not known before'[115] recurs throughout James's empirical research, and the research of others. One finds in these reports, moreover, the widespread claim that the noetic element involved in such instances more closely resembles an increased breadth and depth of insight than forms of comprehension garnered through scientific inquiry, for example, and that belief in the factuality of theism is related closely to these 'states of religious insight into depth of truth unplumbed by the discursive intellect.'[116] Once again, the notion of insight moves to the fore.

Such states of religious insight are not without analogy to incidents in more common everyday life. Facts about the world are often asserted on the basis of insights which are enormously difficult to justify, or even to describe well, as I brought out earlier in this chapter in connection with Murdoch's thought, and with James's account of the idiosyncratic reasonableness to individuals of live propositions. James himself notes the sometimes surprising emergence of such insights, observing the many instances in which 'we have a thought, or we perform an act, repeatedly, but on a certain day the real meaning of the thought peals through us for the first time, or the act has suddenly turned into a moral responsibility.'[117] In the longer term, decades of parenting or teaching or poverty or sickness, for example, bring with them in thoughtful persons a depth, breadth, and distinctiveness of understanding of particular phenomena which underwrite many factual claims in such areas which are extremely difficult to justify satisfactorily to critics.

Phenomena of this kind reported widely in James's empirical work raise a significant philosophical challenge. Canons of empirical justification, it is reported on a wide scale, do not function well in relation to such insight, or to the beliefs occasioned by them, as Dickinson Miller complained in connection with James's epistemology. This raises significant questions about the appropriate scope of application of conventional canons of empirical justification, such as those presupposed by Clifford. To *assume* that such canons are applicable to the experiences recorded in *The Varieties of Religious Experience*, and in many other places, would beg the question raised by the claims of the subjects involved in those studies. There is no scholarly consensus regarding a resolution of the epistemological challenges raised by the ongoing standoff between these two widely attested intellectual phenomena: the success of conventional empirical standards of evidential justification in many compartments of the intellectual relationship between human beings and the world, and a consistent challenge of those standards, on a very widespread scale, in religious and other domains.

One should, of course, be wary of attempts by anyone to justify claims of fact based on privileged, private experience, and James shows himself eager in *The Varieties of Religious Experience* to hold that even widely attested reports can make no claim on persons who have not been privy to the experiences involved. This does not, however, diminish the philosophical demands that are placed by such phenomena upon the philosopher who purports to take empiricism seriously. The scope of live theism historically and socially, which has consistently given rise to such reports, is arresting. It cuts across intellectual, social, political, economic, linguistic, gender, and other lines, and has done so on an extraordinary historical scale. While diverse, and revealing the imprint of the subjects who report them, the historical records of these experiences, and the intellectual claims arising out of them, exhibit no greater diversity and personal influence, as James argues in *The Varieties of Religious Experience*, than the history of philosophy. Such experiences, moreover, are congruent with an exceedingly long *fides quaerens intellectum* tradition of philosophy running continuously from Augustine and before, to Anselm and Aquinas and many philosophers today.

What does this extraordinary scope, depth, and tenacity mean? What it means will be decided very differently depending on the position that one takes on the issue of whether these phenomena may reflect a commensurateness between human beings and the world. James's position on this matter has been poorly understood, and the failure to fully appreciate his argument has contributed to sustaining his reputation as a fideist. The affective consequences of theism spring uniquely from the belief that theism is *true*. Whether or not it is true, however, I left up in the air, pledging to return to it, which I shall now do.

It must be acknowledged, as Russell pointed out, that even false beliefs can generate real personal results. Live theism, in other words, could conceivably involve false belief but could still have essentially the same personal consequences as would be the case if it were true. It is possible, in other words, that theism is false, and that the strenuous mood is a function of a false belief. Certainly James did not deny such a possibility. On the contrary, he willingly conceded that religious experiences, and the invigorating results of them 'may be nothing but ... [the subject's] subjective way of feeling things, a mood of his own fancy, in spite of the effects produced.'[118] It is fashionable after Freud, Feuerbach, and Nietzsche to interpret the phenomenon which James designates as the strenuous mood in this way, and there are powerful arguments which lend favour to this position.

These are not decisive arguments historically, however, as continuing debate makes clear, and so we are once again forced to return to the risk element which James argues cannot be avoided by *any* philosopher. James's position, I have shown, is geared to understanding the significance of *abandoning* a belief state which presently occasions certain unique personal and intellectual consequences. What would constitute responsible behaviour in relation to such a state, James asks, in view of the fact that its abandonment would bring about the loss of the strenuous mood in both its personal and intellectual aspects?

As I indicated, James does not question the permissibility of adopting Clifford's position. What he attacks is the *presumption* that the adoption of that position avoids the risks involved in taking the opposite course, and sustaining a live theism. There is no less risk in overturning a live theism, and losing the strenuous mood which uniquely attends it, than there is in acquiescing in that theism and in that mood, with its personal and intellectual effects. Given the complexity of the intellectual life, and unresolved issues involving various aspects of that life, there is no neutral frame of reference from which one could respond to this challenge and avoid any risk. This will remain the case as long, as Myers has observed, as 'no established discipline can give a straightforward definition'[119] of the need-to-believe phenomenon which clarifies once and for all the degree to which that phenomenon does or does not involve a commensurateness between the human being and the world. It is an uncritical and unwarranted cultural presumption which ignores this fact, James argues, and construes Clifford's position as the safe and responsible one. What needs to be amplified here is the issue of how we are to respond to the possibility that there may exist a commensurateness between ourselves and the world, in which case the marks of live theism would have profound evidential significance. The willingness to go 'half way' in according benefit of the doubt to live theism involves more than just intellectual openness and responsibility in this instance. It also involves the basic metaphysical issue about a possible commensurateness between persons and world. To deny benefit of the doubt to the distinctive characteristics of live theism would have serious implications if those phenomena turned out in the long run to reflect a commensurateness between persons and world which is as yet poorly understood. If this did turn out to be the case, the phenomena typical of live theism would have important epistemological significance, as Myers has observed of James's position.

> The fundamental premise upon which his philosophy of religion rested was that our subjective nature, feelings, emotions, and propensities exist as they do because something in reality harmonizes with them; in so far as they are yearnings and longings, reality will ultimately fulfil them.[120]

If such commensurateness were an entirely hypothetical postulate, one could reasonably conclude, with Myers, returning to wishful thinking charges, that 'no philosopher has ever proposed a more outrageous premise for faith than this. Because we want the world to be a certain way, our desire actually makes it so.[121]

What James actually held, however, is that within the terms of reference of immediate experience as a whole, the postulation of such commensurateness is not entirely gratuitous. What immediate experience makes evident is that there is in fact a confirmable commensurateness between persons and world at a variety of experiential levels. Subjective states, moreover, as well as sensory and certain intellectual ones, are most often treated in a way which assumes such commensurateness. We do not regard disdainful ridicule of persons with alzheimers disease, for example, or raucous laughter at disasters, as fitting responses to certain states of affairs in the world. More generally, the notion that particular states and objects in the world are deserving of fitting subjective as well as intellectual responses, while under strident siege in recent times, has deep roots in the Western philosophical tradition.[122]

Questions about the *scope* of commensurateness between persons and world, a matter which has been subject to debate within epistemology, and particularly among externalists, and within the philosophy of religion in Alvin Plantinga's work,[123] for example, are inescapable when deciding what would constitute a responsible reception of the distinctive characteristics of live theism. Myers seems to hold, with Clifford, that it would be better to proceed on the assumption that the scope of commensurateness does not extend sufficiently far to justify imputing evidential significance to the distinctive states involved in live theism. Why, James asks pointedly, however, would such a position involve any less a gamble than his own, which gives the benefit of the doubt to commensurateness? On what basis would it be advisable to discount the evidential significance of certain aspects of immediate experience on the *presumption* that such a commensurateness does not exist?

It is advisable to proceed this way, Clifford would respond, because it reduces the risk of error. Where, however, James rightly asks, does Clifford show that the most productive road in inquiry is also necessarily always the safest one? We are perfectly entitled to adopt Clifford's position, James emphasizes, and to discount a possible broad commensurateness, as well as certain beliefs or propensities to believe. It may turn out in the long run that we were wise to have done so. If, however, with Clifford, we make such a decision, we do so 'at our peril as much as if we believed.'[124] If it should turn out to be the case that it is only through an experience of the world which accords epistemological significance to distinctive experiential states, that a particular dimension of commensurateness between persons and world can be discovered, then the *a priori* discounting of those states would permanently preclude the discovery of any such commensurateness. If it should turn out, that is, that rationality and religiosity involve a commensurateness with the world which is of such a nature that it is only through acquiescence in an existing live theism that theism's intellectual merits could be gradually uncovered, then Clifford's call for the abandonment of live theism would turn out to have been 'irrational.'[125]

This is James's main point against Clifford, made in connection with James's distinction between fear of error and pursuit of truth:

> This feeling [involved in live theism], forced on us we know not whence, that by obstinately believing that there are gods ... we are doing the universe the deepest service we can, seems part of the living essence of the religious hypothesis. If the hypothesis were true in all its parts, including this one, then pure intellectualism, with its veto on our making willing advances, would be an absurdity; and some participation of our sympathetic nature would be logically required. I, therefore, for one, cannot see my way to accepting the agnostic rules for truth-seeking, or wilfully agree to keep my willing nature out of the game. I cannot do so for this plain reason, that a role of thinking which would absolutely prevent me from acknowledging certain kinds of truth if those kinds of truth were really there, would be an irrational rule.[126]

The challenge of how to respond to the distinctive characteristics of live theism, then, is a twofold one. It involves an intellectual openness and responsibility which accepts the tension between the conflicting elements of the live religious option, and which resists what James saw as the growing social propensity to dismiss the theistic element of that dialectic out of hand. It also, however, inescapably involves a fundamental metaphysical issue:

> A critic may grant James's plea for religious tolerance and thus respect his right-to-believe without granting any rationality to the need-to-believe ... The Jamesean philosophy of religion sometimes appears to accept the separation of paths between believers and nonbelievers, and at other times insists upon having the last word.

James seems to have held that the need-to-believe is mystically inherent in the world and therefore is *inherently rational*. Just when the critic thinks that the impasse has been mutually recognized and that further dialogue is useless, he must challenge the Jamesean again to protest the parting shot. His sympathy may have been elicited for the genuine need-to-believe, but having granted that its causes and effects warrant investigating, he cannot in good conscience agree that it is a rational need. (emphasis added)[127]

James would not try to force on his opponent the view that the distinctive experience of live theism is 'inherently rational,' but he would tenaciously resist any view which *assumes* that it is not, and rightly so. The distinctive characteristics of live theism may turn out to involve rationality in as yet unfathomed ways, some of which are speculated about in the Conclusion of *The Varieties of Religious Experience*. This would have important implications with respect to the form that intellectually responsible behaviour should currently take in relation to live theism. In the present, however, we are not privy to the information we need in this respect, and so we are forced to make a choice which cannot be fully justified empirically, although it is not entirely without justification. It is a choice, however, which James rightly sees as unavoidable in a consistent *evidentialism*. It is not a fideistic gamble which from the outset surrenders all aspirations to evidence, nor does it necessarily open the door to wishful thinking. It is, rather, a prerequisite of responsibly pursuing truth, given the possibility that truth may turn out to involve a commensurateness between persons and world of wider scope than we presently understand.

*The Varieties of Religious Experience, Radical Empiricism, The Will to Believe,* and many other works exhibit Radical Empiricism's characteristic aversion to premature closure of any questions, particularly those raised in the foregoing pages. James's thought exhibits a deep reticence about the cultural propensity to beg such questions by automatically privileging conventional canons of evidentially responsible behaviour without due regard for the magnitude of the challenge to those very canons which is created by such a widespread and long-lived phenomenon as live theism. It would not be an exaggeration to say that this reticence is the primary force behind *The Will to Believe*, as well as *The Varieties of Religious Experience*, as I have argued.

James's defence of belief rather than the nonbelieving state is more an exhibition of his determination not to beg the question at this level than it is a partisan sponsoring of theism, much less a promotion of fideism. It is an exhibition of exactly the kind of empirical rigor, and resistance to premature claims to comprehensiveness, for which James was commended even by Russell in his critical analysis of pragmatism. Here, the distinctive character of James's Radical Empiricism plays an important role in appreciating the nature of his position. As I indicated at the beginning of this book, and have underscored on a number of occasions, such a tradition holds the empiricist responsible for taking into account, in forming epistemological theory, and developing norms of responsible doxastic behaviour, *all* the relevant phenomena accessible to us, *as* they are found. Many commentators, embracing a less rigorous form of empiricism, have missed the crucial role that Radical Empiricism plays in James's philosophy of religion, and as a result have misinterpreted him as fideistic.

It is in the spirit of Radical Empiricism that James resists overturning live theism on Clifford's grounds. Choices have to be made about the epistemological significance of the noetic elements of the theistic belief state, and those choices will lead to different outcomes regarding judgments about what constitutes intellectually responsible behaviour in relation to live theism. James's aim in his philosophy of religion is to protect *all* such differences of opinion from the vagaries of intellectual fashion, and particularly, as I indicated, from what he saw as a growing cultural propensity to spontaneously deny benefit of the doubt to religious phenomena. He was rightly unwilling to allow questions about the full scope of what constitutes rational behaviour to be considered settled as long as the foregoing disputes continued.

I have argued in this chapter against prudential readings of James, and against the accusations that he confused belief and hypothesis-adoption. I have done so based largely upon what he says about the strenuous mood, and upon what can be further inferred about that mood from *The Varieties of Religious Experience*. James was very clear that it was the belief state which needed to be defended, for the strenuous mood is uniquely related to that state. He was equally clear that even the aspects of the strenuous mood which are desirable would not and could not enable or justify the creation of the form of belief which engenders that mood. James did not hold that the cultivation of theistic belief is justified by its edifying personal benefits, in this sense. It would have made no sense for him to counsel the adoption of religious belief solely in order to secure its edifying personal consequences, when his account of the moral life and the strenuous mood so prominently precludes such a position, both implicitly and explicitly, as I have shown. In all this, his position is consistent, coherent and sound.

Prudential readings such as Wernham's subordinate the strenuous mood to the terms of reference of the individual's own narrowly personal and self-serving ambitions for affective edification alone, whereas the Jamesean strenuous mood is a byproduct of a self-abandoning allegiance to a 'greater ideal'[128] than personal edification. I have shown James to have held that the domination of one's intellectual life by narrowly self-interested terms of reference would preclude precisely the emergence of the strenuous mood, as he understands it. Paradoxically, the prudential motivation to secure the exclusively personal, beneficial consequences of theism for one's own individual advantage involves a narrowness which is so deeply at odds with the self-forgetful posture of the strenuous mood that this motivation is by itself an insuperable impediment to the attainment of this mood. The paradox of the strenuous mood is that the narrowing of perspective occasioned by seeking its affective component alone, entirely for one's individual, personal benefit, is utterly antithetical to the personal motivation, the particular intellectual horizon, and the noetic elements of the strenuous mood. Hick was right to attack a prudential argument as vigorously as he did. He was wrong, however, in taking James to have advanced this argument.

It is only within the terms of reference of the moral life as described in this chapter that James's notion of the strenuous mood can be properly understood, and that charges against him for having endorsed wishful thinking, and confused belief and hypothesis-adoption, can be properly assessed. The strenuous mood is an amplification of the processes which constitute the moral life. The strenuous mood invigorates the pursuit of moral discernment; it heightens the *urgency* with which on 'attends' to certain moral insights, with commensurate effects upon behaviour. This attentiveness is a function of the melioristic belief, not just conjecture, that there are enormous consequences for this world, and the human beings in it, of the decisions made by free human agents in collaboration with the divine. It involves decisions about the evidential significance of the experiential elements of live theism, and a clear recognition that there is no philosophical position which can escape making choices on this matter which are not fully justified.

In the end, even Wernham, who is one of the few commentators to consider the strenuous mood in connection with prudential interpretations of James's position and the belief/hypothesis-adoption issue, turns out to be wide of the mark. To think of the strenuous mood primarily as a desirable state, detachable from melioristic and religious beliefs, which ought prudentially to be pursued in the self-interested desire for its personally beneficial effects, is untenable on all counts. The strenuous mood is a quality which accrues to the moral life under certain circumstances, a quality which suffuses the fundamental and irreducible unity of intellect, volition, affect, agency, and character which I have tried to show as involved together in the pursuit of moral discernment, and the behaviour which attends such discernment. Future attempts to sustain prudential interpretations of James, and attack him for confusing belief and hypothesis-adoption, must take account of the strenuous mood. However, I cannot see how these longstanding interpretations and criticisms of James can be sustained.

# Conclusion

Throughout the last century, James has been widely understood to have proposed a prudential argument sponsoring a fideistic movement ahead of evidence in the adoption of religious belief. I have argued that a closer analysis of liveness, of the details of exactly what consequences James held to flow from live theism, and the role of the subject within the context of immediate experience as a whole, seriously undermines such a reception of his position. James was concerned principally with what would constitute an appropriate response to an existing phenomenon, live theism, with the personal as well as the intellectual elements of the strenuous mood to which live theism gives rise. James never contended that the creation of a belief, religious or otherwise, is justified on prudential grounds. On the contrary, in explicit connection with the will to believe doctrine, he disavowed the notion that it is even possible to create a belief, much less that it would be responsible to create one for self-serving purposes. What he defended were certain existing religious convictions, against the background of what he observed in *The Will to Believe, The Varieties of Religious Experience* and elsewhere to be an increasingly entrenched cultural predisposition against theism. These cultural developments, supported by Clifford-like invocations of evidence *per se,* greatly underestimate the interrelation of the many influences involved in live propositions, especially in belief systems as complex as theism.

The role for subjectivity commended by James, and the significance which he assigned to the consequences of live theism,
were understood by him within the terms of reference of this
complexity. Such complexity involves in a central way what
John Wild has termed a 'double intentionality' wherein subject
and world are simultaneously implicated in the constitution of
experience, albeit in a way which often precludes a clear, introspective disentangling of their respective roles. 'Does the river
make its banks, or do the banks make the river?' as James put it;
'does a man walk with his right leg or with his left leg more
essentially? Just as impossible may it be to separate the real from
the human factors in the growth of our cognitive experience.'[1]

This complex interrelation lies at the heart of James's account
of liveness in *The Will to Believe*. I have also argued that the diffi-
culties involved in introspectively disentangling subject and
world do not lead to the subjectivism and the wishful thinking
with which James has traditionally been charged. Intellectual
inventiveness and passional nature have a physical, metaphysical, social, cultural, linguistic and historical setting, all of which
are constitutive of immediate experience. These elements play
restrictive roles in relation to each other even when the exact
nature of the roles is not always distinguishable through introspection. Pragmatism's appeals to utility and workability,
involving *all* the available consequences of particular conceptions and beliefs, are advanced within these terms of reference.

These terms of reference also provide the setting for James's
contention that there may be a congeniality between the knower
and the world which would make the distinctive characteristics
of live theism epistemologically significant. These conditions
impede any indiscriminate invocation of such congeniality for
the purposes of appealing solely to personal desire as justification for religious or any other kinds of belief. This position is
directly relevant not only to the philosophy of religion, but to
what is still today, a century after *The Will to Believe*, the ongoing
epistemological effort to find a philosophical escape route from
the perennial oscillation between 'a coherentism that threatens to disconnect thought from reality, and on the other side a
vain appeal to the Given, in the sense of bare presences that

are supposed to constitute the ultimate grounds of empirical judgments.'[2]

Because James's philosophy of religion looks to his position on immediate experience as a whole, future analyses of his thought on religion should be directed more extensively towards that aspect of his work. It is time to stop isolating the subject, and proceeding to rehearse the now-familiar general broadsides against subjectivism, wishful thinking, and so on, which seem to follow the reflective compartmentalization of experience. What is needed is more careful inquiry into James's account of immediate experience and its significance with respect to the involvement of passional nature in doxastic practice. If James has succeeded in integrating into his epistemology the subject and her community, with its cultural history, institutions, language, practices, and so on, without excluding a regulative influence on all these by the world itself, as I believe he did, then many of the traditional charges against him must be seriously reevaluated.

If one locates James's philosophy of religion within the terms of immediate experience, it is readily apparent that he defended live theism because it is experienced by actual individuals and communities as *reasonable*, and because intellectual responsibility – and an empiricism worthy of the name – demand respect for such reasonableness. What is 'evident' to an individual or culture is to a significant extent a contextual matter, that involves the foregoing constellation of historical, linguistic, cultural, temperamental, physical and other influences which cannot be ignored in the development of evidential standards that are practically meaningful. What is 'evident' to the individual or community, however, is not entirely a contextual matter. James's historicizing and contextualizing of inquiry intended to emphasize not only the fragmentary and provisional nature of all claims to truth, but to give a place in epistemology to the recalcitrance of experience in its actual historical occurrence – a recalcitrance which often flies in the face of 'wayward personal standards.' In my view he achieves a great deal of success in this endeavour.

This feature of James's thought ought to have become apparent in his repeated assertions of allegiance to the pursuit of objectivity in belief, and to evidential responsibility, as I have argued. The juxtaposition of allegiance to both objectivity and contextualization does not reflect inconsistency on his part. It manifests, rather, his attentiveness to the diversity of influences which *together* generate the experience of reasonableness. Intellectual considerations are no less important than existential ones in the constitution of reasonableness. As Myers said:

> when it goes very well it is as if thinking and living have merged into a single, harmonious, and vibrant process, as if thinking has found its goal in a newfound health of experiencing ... By making his own mental pictures reflect the unimpeded flow of pure experience, James felt a restoration, through thought itself, of a healthful fluency of thought that is the mark of rationality.[3]

James defended theism above all because, for him, and for other intellectually competent and responsible persons, it possessed this 'mark of rationality.' Such reasonableness was not taken by him to furnish a knock-down vindication of theism; nor was it taken to provide any guarantee that an intrusion of self-interest would not be involved in religious belief to some degree. What he argued, with respect to theism and many other beliefs, is that it is their reasonableness which guides the highly fallible, ongoing search for the truth. Only the continued embrace of such existing beliefs would eventually reveal the manner in which their embodiment in immediate experience would effect 'the character with which life concretely comes,' as he was seen previously to have put it, 'and the expression which it bears of being, or at least of involving, a muddle and struggle, with an "ever not quite" to all our formulas, and novelty and possibility forever leaking in.'[4] This is a historical and social process, James emphasized, as much as it is an individual and reflective one. It is a process ultimately guided by *existing* concepts and beliefs together with an openness to their potential inadequacies.

With this depiction, James bears a closer family resemblance to a number of contemporary non-fideistic philosophers of religion than to the prudential fideists with whom he is more often associated. There is a significant resemblance, for example, between James's position and the positions held by some contemporary philosophers regarding epistemically 'basic' beliefs. Discussion of what constitutes a properly basic belief is extensive. One common theme, however, as Nicholas Woltersdorff has put it, is that 'the proper way to arrive at ... a criterion [of basicality] is, broadly speaking, inductive.'[5] This way requires looking to certain *existing* beliefs in the process of producing a criterion of proper basicality, rather than beginning with the criteria of classical foundationalism, for example, which Plantinga, Sosa and others have shown to have serious shortcomings. Norms of basicality should be developed from 'below,' as it were, avoiding what William Alston has deplored as the 'epistemic imperialism' involved in the indiscriminate application of certain abstract standards of basicality. Such standards, he and many others argue, prematurely exclude claims to the reasonableness of certain widely existing beliefs, including theism, and dismiss prematurely the possibility of the proper basicality of such beliefs.[6] Louis Dupré, approaching the issue differently from Reformed epistemologists, has also argued in favour of affording actual theism an initial benefit of the doubt, urging a recognition, to use Henry Dumery's words, that 'the philosopher *encounters* this idea [of God]; he is not the author of it. He must therefore seek to know what it signifies and what role in life can be assigned to it.'[7] In the expanded version of his 1986-87 Gifford Lectures, John Hick proposes an account of theistic 'natural belief'[8] which he recognizes to have a kinship with Penelhum's 'parity argument,' to similar effect,[9] and which stands in this contemporary tradition of thought.

Many additional examples from current epistemological debate could be added, but the pattern of appeal to existing experiences, beliefs and practices in the determination of proper criteria for what constitutes properly basic beliefs is clear. The centrality of 'liveness' in James's thought, within the context of his work on immediate experience, seems to me to align itself with such contemporary work. This is not to say that his position is identical with the views of the foregoing philosophers.

He is more individualistic than some (Alston), more anti-institutional than others (Dupré), and less technically developed in relation to traditional foundationalism (Plantinga).

All these philosophers, however, and many others, share a commitment to inquire further into the widely reported reasonableness of live theism in its actual occurrence. Whether Alston's internalist/externalist approach, or Plantinga's Warrant and Proper Function, or the empirical and historical inquiries of Dupré, or Zagzebski's virtue epistemology, or other positions will carry the day is not yet clear. Whatever the outcome, however, it is respect for the as yet unfathomed phenomenon of live theism, in its actual occurrence, which plays a central role in the work of all these philosophers, and it is with this direction of contemporary thought that I wish to align James through my attention to his account of liveness, the strenuous mood, and immediate experience. A clearer recognition of this alignment should contribute to James being drawn more effectively into current conversation than has hitherto been the case.

# Notes

## Introduction

1 William James, '1903 Notebook,' R.B. Perry, in *The Thought and Character of William James*, 2 vols. (Boston: Little, Brown, 1935), 2: 700.
2 William James, *The Will to Believe and Other Essays in Popular Philosophy* (Cambridge: Harvard University Press, 1979), 6.
3 Ibid.
4 William Kingdom Clifford, *Lectures and Essays* (London: MacMillan and Co., 1886), 344.
5 Ibid., 343. See also 346 and 359.
6 James, 'Will to Believe,' 6.
7 Richard Taylor, introduction to *Theism* by John Stuart Mill (Indianapolis: Bobbs-Merrill, 1957), xv.
8 James, 'Will to Believe,' 101.
9 Morton White, 'Pragmatism and the Revolt against Formalism: Revising Some Doctrines of William James,' *Transactions of the Charles S. Peirce Society*, 26 (1990), 15. See also Walter Kaufmann, *Critique of Religion and Philosophy* (Garden City: Anchor Books, 1961), 114–20; Wallace Matson, *The Existence of God* (Ithaca: Cornell University Press, 1965), 206–15.
10 Bertrand Russell, *History of Western Philosophy* (London: George Allen and Unwin, 1961); *Philosophical Essays* (New York: Longmans, Green, 1910); James Wernham, *James's Will-to-Believe Doctrine: A Heretical View* (Kingston and Montreal: McGill-Queen's University Press, 1987).

## 1: The Woodpecker and the Grub

1 There is controversy about the relation between James's earlier pragmatism and his later radical empiricism. This matter will be addressed later in the book.

2 William James, *Essays in Radical Empiricism and A Pluralistic Universe* (New York: Longmans, Green, 1942), 42.

3 Louis Dupré, *The Other Dimension: A Search for the Meaning of Religious Attitudes.* (New York: Doubleday, 1972), 126–7.

4 William James, *The Varieties of Religious Experience: A Study in Human Nature* (Cambridge: Harvard University Press, 1985), 30.

5 Ibid., 39.

6 William James, *Pragmatism* (Cambridge: Harvard University Press, 1975), 57.

7 Ibid., 57–8.

8 Ibid., 58.

9 Ibid.

10 Ibid., 57.

11 Ibid., 56.

12 Ibid., 58.

13 James, *Varieties of Religious Experience*, 399.

14 Ibid., 398.

15 This is particularly relevant in relation to current disputes among philosophers of religion of analytic and hermeneutical persuasions. See William J. Wainwright, ed. *God, Philosophy, and Academic Culture* (Atlanta: Scholars Press, 1996).

16 James, *Varieties of Religious Experience*, 407–8.

17 R. Otto, *The Idea of the Holy*, tr. John W. Harvey (London: Oxford University Press, 1923).

18 James, *Varieties of Religious Experience*, 397.

19 Ibid., 406.

20 James, *Pluralistic Universe*, 311. When he says 'either in power or in knowledge,' it is the former which is most significant in James's position overall. For present summary purposes, then, I will take James's challenge of traditional theology here to be primarily a challenge of divine omnipotence.

21 Ibid. See also *Varieties of Religious Experience*, 413.

22 There are longstanding scholarly debates about the relation

between the 'God of the Bible' and the 'God of the philosophers' on the issue of divine involvement in the world, the effect of such involvement on the world, and on God. Much work in various denominational areas is being done in this connection. James was well aware of some core issues involved in this subject long before these more recent initiatives. He observes, for example, that

the theistic conception, picturing God and his creation as entities distinct from each other, still leaves the human subject outside of the deepest reality in the universe. God is from eternity complete, it says, and sufficient unto himself; he throws off the world by a free act and as an extraneous substance, and he throws off man as a third substance, extraneous to both the world and himself ... An orthodox theism has been so jealous of God's glory that it has taken pains to exaggerate everything in the notion of him that could make for isolation and separateness. Page upon page in scholastic books go to prove that God is in no sense implicated by his creative act, or involved in his creation. That his relation to the creatures he has made should make any difference to him, carry any consequence, or qualify his being, is repudiated as a pantheistic slur upon his self-sufficingness ... His action can affect us, but he can never be affected by our reaction ... This essential dualism of the theistic view has all sorts of collateral consequences. Man being an outsider and a mere subject to God, not his intimate partner, a character of externality invades the field. *Pluralistic Universe*, 25–7

23  James, *Varieties of Religious Experience*, 400.
24  James, *Pragmatism*, 136–7.
25  Ibid., 135.
26  Ibid., 55.
27  James, *Pluralistic Universe*, 114.
28  James, *Pragmatism*, 40.
29  Ibid.
30  Ibid.
31  Ibid.
32  James, *Pluralistic Universe*, 114.
33  Ibid.
34  James, *Pragmatism*, 139.

35  Ibid., 142.
36  James, *Varieties of Religious Experience*, 174.
37  Letter of W. James to Mark Baldwin, 1899, Perry, *Thought and Character*, 2: 243.
38  James, *Varieties of Religious Experience*, 411.
39  James, *Pragmatism*, 58.
40  Ibid., 44.
41  Ibid.
42  Ibid., 56.

**2: The Will to Believe**

1  William James, 'The Will to Believe,' *New World* 5 (1896), 327–47.
2  James, 'The Will to Believe,' in *The Will to Believe and Other Essays in Popular Philosophy* (New York: Longmans, Green, 1897).
3  James, 'The Will to Believe,' in *Selected Papers on Philosophy* (London: Dent and Co., New York: E.P. Dutton, 1917).
4  William James, 'Review of *The Unseen Universe*,' *Nation*, 20 (1875): 366–7.
5  Madden, 'Introduction' to *The Will to Believe and Other Essays in Popular Philosophy*, by William James, xviii–xix.
6  Letter of C. Wright to Grace Norton, 12 July 1875, in Perry, *Thought and Character*, 1: 530–2.
7  Ibid., 531.
8  Even Hare and Kauber, who argue that this apparent retreat from the original association of duty with belief was a mistake on James's part, admit that there is no evidence that James maintained a doctrine of a duty to believe after 1875. (Kauber and Hare, 'The Right and Duty to Will to Believe,' *Canadian Journal of Philosophy*, 4 (1974): 327–43.
9  Letter of W. James to Mark Baldwin, 1899, in Perry, *Thought and Character*, 2: 243.
10  Letter of W. James to Mark Baldwin, 24 Oct. 1901, in Perry, *Thought and Character*, 2: 244.
11  Letter of W. James to L.T. Hobhouse, 12 Aug. 1904, in Perry, *Thought and Character*, 2: 245.
12  James, *The Will to Believe and Other Essays in Popular Philosophy*, 254. See also Kauber and Hare, 'Right and Duty,' 330.

13 James, 'Will to Believe,' 88.
14 Kauber and Hare, 'Right and Duty,' 327.
15 Letter of C.S. Peirce to W. James, 9 March 1909, in Perry, *Thought and Character*, 2: 438.
16 Gail Kennedy, 'Pragmatism, Pragmaticism, and the Will to Believe – A Reconsideration,' *The Journal of Philosophy*, 55 (1958): 583.
17 John Hick, *Faith and Knowledge* (London: Macmillan, 1967), 32–56.
18 Ibid., 34. Hick's work in this respect has the distinctive merit of relating James's position to Pascal's, whereas most commentators have remained preoccupied with its relation to Clifford. I will undertake a closer analysis of the relation between the positions of James and Pascal.
19 Ibid., 40.
20 Ibid., 35.
21 Ibid., 44.
22 Ibid., 42.
23 Ibid., 44.
24 Russell, *Philosophical Essays*, 189.
25 Russell, *History of Western Philosophy*, 770.
26 Letter of Mark Baldwin to W. James, 1899, in Perry, *Thought and Character*, 2: 242.
27 Russell, *Philosophical Essays*, 189.
28 Wernham, *Heretical*, 3, 101. 'If it is about belief at all, it is what Price has called an "economics" of belief.'
29 Ibid., 3.
30 Dickinson Miller, 'James's Doctrine of "The Right to Believe,"' *The Philosophical Review*, 51 (1942): 548.
31 Ibid., 547.
32 Ibid.
33 Ibid., 548.
34 Ibid.
35 Ibid., 547.
36 Ibid., 546. In his correspondence with Benjamin Paul Blood James describes truth in these terms, referring to 'lightning flashes, darting gleams ... that's the way truth is' (letter of W. James to Benjamin Blood, 28 April 1897, in Perry, *Thought and Character*, 2: 234). This

aspect of James's position becomes more central in later chapters of this book in connection with the centrality of metaphor in James's epistemology.

37 Ibid., 551.

38 Ibid.

39 Ibid.

40 Ibid., 553.

41 Ibid., 546.

42 Ibid., 552.

43 Ibid., 546.

44 Ibid.

45 Before passing on to James's response to his critics, it should be noted that some commentators have conceded the wishful thinking charges but tried to rescue James from philosophical culpability for having proposed a position which moves in such a direction. Stephen Davis, for example, portrays James as having separated subjective states from intellectual ones, and as having made the former serve as grounds for belief in a way which amounts to an endorsement of wishful thinking. Davis, however, defends such a position arguing that wishful thinking is necessary under the conditions set out in James's essay. See Stephen Davis, 'Wishful Thinking and "The Will to Believe,"' *Transactions of the Charles S. Peirce Society* 8 (1972), 237. James Muyskens also interprets James as having defended a 'very liberal or weak standard for justified belief' which 'verges on the irresponsible' sufficiently to be susceptible of charges of wishful thinking. Muyskens also attempts to rescue James by suggesting that 'instead of seeing James's task as the attempt to justify the belief that p, we can ... reasonably reinterpret his remarks to be an attempt to justify hope that p,' a position which 'does not require giving up the strong Lockean criterion of justified belief.' See James Muyskens, 'James's Defense of a Believing Attitude in Religion,' *Transactions of the Charles S. Peirce Society* (Winter, 1974), 53.

46 Letter of W. James to Mark Baldwin, 1901, in Perry, *Thought and Character*, 2: 243.

47 F.H. Bradley, 'On Truth and Practice,' *Mind*, 13 (1904); A.E. Taylor, 'Some Side Lights on Pragmatism,' *The McGill University Magazine*, 3 (1903–4). See Perry, *Thought and Character*, 2: 246.

48 L.T. Hobhouse, 'Faith and the Will to Believe,' in *Proceedings of the Aristotelian Society,* 4 (1904): 91, 104–5, 109. See Perry, *Thought and Character,* 2: 245.

49 Letter of W. James to L.T. Hobhouse, 12 Aug. 1904, in Perry, *Thought and Character,* 2: 245. It is worth noting here James's rarely acknowledged insistence upon locating the individual's belief-formation activities within a social context, as I will bring out later in the book. *The Will to Believe,* says James, 'treated the faith-attitude as a necessity for individuals, because the total "evidence," which only the race can draw, has to include their experiments among its data' (ibid.). In a 1907 letter, James insisted again on social considerations when dealing with the individual's belief-formation processes (letter of W. James to H.M. Kallen, in Perry, *Thought and Character,* 2: 249).

50 Letter of W. James to John Chapman, 5 April 1897, in Perry, *Thought and Character,* 2: 237. See Madden, 'Introduction,' xxi.

51 John Dewey, in Kennedy, 'Reconsideration,' 583.

52 Letter of W. James to Horace Kallen, 1 Aug., 1907, Perry, in *Thought and Character,* 2: 249. See Kennedy, 'Reconsideration,' 583–4.

53 Kennedy, 'Reconsideration,' 587.

54 Ibid.

55 Madden, 'Introduction,' xxiii.

56 Ibid., xxx–viii.

57 Ibid., xviii.

58 Ibid., xxiii, xxiv.

59 Ibid., xv–xvi.

60 Kennedy, 'Reconsideration,' 580.

61 Letter of F.C.S. Schiller to Charles Strong, in Perry, *Thought and Character,* 2: 241.

62 Ibid. Certain recurrent biographical considerations have also been invoked in connection with the possibility that James had been misunderstood. Madden has cautioned that too much can be made of James's recourse to volition during his psychological crisis of 1870 (Madden, 'Introduction,' xxvii). Other features of James's personality have been brought into consideration as well. Madden, for example, points out that James was not a person who was at all easily disposed temperamentally to believe or make intellectual decisions lightly. On the contrary, he was someone who held back

his intellectual assent until much inquiry had taken place and until much argument, if not evidence, had been marshalled (ibid., xxiii).

One ought not to overlook as well the effect upon the reception of James's essay of its rhetorical character. James's addresses were closely geared to the public circumstances of their delivery. He was chided by his friend, Benjamin Paul Blood, for example, for the 'oratorical effect' of such lectures (Letter of Benjamin Blood to W. James, 18 April 1897, in Perry, *Thought and Character*, 2: 233). The rhetorical and non-technical character of those lectures has not always been taken adequately into account by commentators. Some years after delivering *The Will to Believe*, corresponding with L.T. Hobhouse, James observed that 'each man writes from out of a field of consciousness of which the bogey in the background is the chief object' (letter of W. James to L.T. Hobhouse, 12 Aug., 1904, in Perry, *Thought and Character*, 2: 246). It is crucial to clarify what bogey was involved in *The Will to Believe*. James's bogey was the spectre of a widespread and growing antagonism towards religious belief which denied to belief even the preliminary benefit of the doubt to which James thought it was entitled.

63  Letter of W. James to Mark Baldwin, 1899, in Perry, *Thought and Character*, 2: 243.
64  James, 'Will to Believe,' 105.
65  Ibid., 106.
66  Ibid., 88.
67  Letter of W. James to Mark Baldwin, 1899, in Perry, *Thought and Character*, 2: 243.
68  James, 'Will to Believe,' 91.
69  Ibid., 93.
70  Ibid., 95.
71  Ibid., 102.
72  Ibid., 103.
73  Ibid., 107.
74  Ibid., 88.
75  Ibid., 108.
76  Ibid., 107.
77  Ibid., 106.
78  Ibid., 107.

79  Ibid.
80  Ibid.
81  Ibid., 108.
82  Letter of W. James to Mark Baldwin, 1899, in Perry, *Thought and Character*, 2: 244.
83  James, 'Will to Believe,' 109.
84  Ibid., 95.
85  Ibid., 107.
86  Ibid., 100.
87  See Arthur O. Lovejoy, 'The Thirteen Pragmatisms. I and II,' *The Journal of Philosophy*, 5 (January, 1908): 5–12, 29–39; Paul Henle, 'William James: Introduction,' in Max H. Fisch, ed., *Classic American Philosophers* (New York: Appleton-Century-Crofts, 1951): 115–27; Robert G. Meyers, 'The Roots of Pragmatism: Madden on James and Peirce,' in *Transactions of the Charles S. Peirce Society*, 25 (Spring, 1989): 85–123; Edward H. Madden, 'Discussing James and Peirce with Meyers,' in *Transactions of the Charles S. Peirce Society*, 25 (Spring, 1989): 123–48.
88  James, 'Will to Believe,' 100.
89  It has been contended that the 'forced' aspect of the options of interest to James in his essay is not even integral to his overall case. George Mavrodes, for example, has argued to this effect, as well as Kauber and Hare who have made an extensive case for the contention that 'while James often spoke in terms of forced options and self-fulfilling beliefs, the right to believe is *not* limited by James to these two categories.' See George Mavrodes, 'James and Clifford on "The Will to Believe,"' in Keith Yandell, ed., *God Man and Religion: Readings in the Philosophy of Religion* (McGraw-Hill, 1973): 524–8; Kauber and Hare, 'Right and Duty,' 334.
90  James, 'Will to Believe,' 90.
91  Ibid.
92  Ibid., 92.
93  Ibid.
94  Ibid.
95  Ibid., 93.
96  Ibid.
97  Ibid., 103.
98  Ibid.

99 Ibid.

100 Ibid.

101 Ibid.

102 Ibid., 98.

103 Ibid., 102.

104 Ibid., 90.

105 Ibid., 93.

106 Ibid., 97.

107 Ibid., 98.

108 Ibid.

109 Ibid., 99. See also 96 and 108.

110 Ibid., 100.

111 Letter of W. James to H.M. Kallen, 1907, in Perry, *Thought and Character*, 2: 249.

112 Ibid.

113 John Wild, *The Radical Empiricism of William James* (Garden City: Doubleday, 1969), 331.

114 Wernham, *Heretical*, 91.

115 James Edie, *William James and Phenomenology* (Bloomington: Indiana University Press, 1987), 32. See also 26.

116 Gerald Myers, *William James: His Life and Thought* (New Haven: Yale University Press, 1986), 276.

117 Edie, *William James and Phenomenology*, 31.

118 Myers, *James: His Life and Thought*, 110. See also 355.

119 Ibid., 130.

120 Ibid., 214.

121 Ibid., 261.

122 Ibid., 263.

123 Ibid., 352–3.

124 Ibid., 563.

125 Ibid., 57–8.

126 Wild, *Radical Empiricism*, 377. See also 366.

127 Edie, *William James and Phenomenology*, 24. See also 46, 73.

128 John J. McDermott, 'introduction' to *The Writings of William James*, xxxiii.

129 Kauber and Hare, 'Right and Duty,' 329. See also 341.

130 Ibid., 329.

131 Edie, *William James and Phenomenology*, 46.

132  William James, *The Principles of Psychology,* 2 vols. (New York: Henry Holt, 1890), I: 264. See also 271.

133  Ibid.

134  Ibid., 269.

135  Ibid., 256.

136  Ibid., 259.

137  Ibid., 269.

138  Ibid., 275.

139  Ibid., 275–6.

140  Ibid., 281.

141  Ibid., 282.

142  Ibid., 276. See also James, *Collected Essays and Reviews* (London: Longmans, Green, 1920), 379.

143  James, *Varieties of Religious Experience,* 189.

144  Iris Murdoch, *The Sovereignty of Good* (London: Ark Paperbacks, 1970).

145  James, *Pragmatism,* 83–4.

146  Ibid., 37.

147  Ibid., 89.

148  Ibid., 36.

149  Ibid., 84.

150  Ibid., 102–3.

151  Ibid., 83.

152  Ibid., 43.

153  See Chapter 13 of *Principles.*

154  James, *Principles,* 2: 630.

155  Ibid.

156  Ibid., 638.

157  Ibid., 633.

158  Ibid., 627.

159  William James, 'The Moral Philosopher and the Moral Life,' in *Essays in Pragmatism,* ed. Alburey Castell (New York: Hafner Publishing, 1948), 67.

160  Ibid.

161  Ibid., 82.

162  James, *Principles,* 2: 636–7.

163  Ibid., 634.

164  Ibid., 637.

165 Ibid.
166 Ibid.
167 Ibid., 639.
168 Ibid., 636.
169 Ibid., 667.
170 Ibid., 639–40.
171 Ibid., 636.
172 Ibid.
173 Ibid., 360.
174 Ibid.
175 Charlene Seigfried, *William James's Radical Reconstruction of Philosophy* (Albany: State University of New York Press, 1990), 161.
176 Ibid., 165.
177 Ibid., 139.
178 Ibid., 169.
179 Ibid., 167.
180 James, 'Will to Believe,' 95.
181 Ibid.

## 3: Subjectivity and Belief

1 Myers, *William James: His Life and Thought*, 461.
2 Ibid.
3 McDermott, introduction to *The Writings of William James*, xxix.
4 Seigfried, *Chaos and Context: A Study in William James* (Athens: Ohio University Press, 1978), 112.
5 James, *Pragmatism*, 125.
6 Ibid.
7 James, *Principles*, 1: 239
8 James, 'Interview in [The] New York Times, 1907,' in McDermott, ed., *The Writings of William James*, 448.
9 Ibid.
10 Madden, Chakrabarti, Meyers and numerous others agree in designating James as a 'naive' or 'natural' realist. See Edward Madden and Chandana Chakrabarti, 'James' "Pure Experience" versus Ayer's "Weak Phenomenalism,"' in *Transactions of the Charles S. Peirce Society* 12 (Winter, 1976), 5, 10. See also Meyers, 'Roots,' 86.
11 James, *Pragmatism*, 96.

12  Ibid., 102.
13  James, *The Meaning of Truth* (Cambridge, Mass.: Harvard University Press, 1975), 3.
14  Ibid. See also James, *Pragmatism*, 96.
15  James, 'Moral Philosopher,' 70.
16  James, *The Meaning of Truth*, 9.
17  James, *Pragmatism*, 120.
18  Ibid., 106–7.
19  Ibid., 111.
20  Ibid., 117.
21  Ibid.
22  James, 'Moral Philosopher,' 81.
23  James, *Pragmatism*, 117.
24  Ibid., 120.
25  Ibid.
26  Ibid., 129.
27  Ibid., 120.
28  Ibid., 117.
29  Ibid., 119.
30  James, *Principles*, 2: 362.
31  'The Pragmatic Theory is a form of cognitive relativism, denying any objective, interest-independent reality, as the proponents of the Correspondence Theory and the Coherence Theory would maintain' (Louis Pojman, *What Can We Know: An Introduction to the Theory of Knowledge* [Belmont, Calif.: Wadsworth, 1995], 327).
32  James, *The Meaning of Truth*, 45.
33  Wild, *Radical Empiricism*, 204.
34  Russell, *Philosophical Essays*, 141.
35  Wild, *Radical Empiricism*, 384.
36  Ibid.
37  Ibid.
38  Ibid.
39  Ibid., 406.
40  Ibid.
41  Seigfried, *Chaos and Context*, 112.
42  Ibid.
43  Edie, *William James and Phenomenology*, 70.
44  Meyers stands apart among participants in the discussion of

James's work, in arguing that the phenomenalist is not committed to an atomistic account of sensory experience which must be augmented by an account of the constructive or interpretive activity of the knower. Phenomenalists differ, according to Meyers, in their views of the degree of unity which exists among sense data as given. Phenomenalists can be understood as falling into both realist and idealist camps. On this basis, Meyers argues that the viability of Ayer's interpretation of James as a strong phenomenalist, for example, has not yet been settled. James's realism can be acknowledged, Meyers thinks, within the terms of reference of a phenomenalistic interpretation of James's overall epistemology. Madden, by contrast, argues that phenomenalism is inherently and necessarily atomistic in its understanding of sense data, and is forced to be either constructivist or interpretive in its understanding of the ways in which atomistic sense data come to be unified in the experience of objects. In most accounts, however, the strong phenomenalist position is representative and constructivist in a way that James's position is not. In strong phenomenalism, a dualism of knower and object is overcome by the relation between the representational construction of sense data and the corresponding object. 'The epistemic problem is to bridge the gulf between physical objects conceived as "theoretical constructs" and their evidential base [consisting of the particulars of sense experience]' (Madden and Chakrabarti, 'Pure Experience,' 13). In James's position on immediate experience, 'there is no "gap" in the first place' (ibid., 8). A dualism of act and object is a retrospective, not an introspective phenomenon. The given, for James, then, 'is much wider in scope than for sense-data philosophers and phenomenalists, including not only patches of color, odors, tastes, etc., but also the entire physical object itself,' as well as relations existing among objects. See A.J. Ayer, *The Origins of Pragmatism* (San Francisco: Freeman, Cooper, 1968). See also Peter H. Hare, and Chandana Chakrabarti, 'The Development of William James's Epistemological Realism,' in Maurice Wohlgelernter, ed., *History, Religion, and Spiritual Democracy* (New York: Columbia, 1980), 238.

45  Myers, *William James: His Life and Thought*, 314.
46  Ibid., 314.
47  James, *Principles*, I: 224.

48 The marginalia of James's library holdings indicate that the atomism of Hume's position much concerned him. See A.A. Roback, *William James: His Marginalia, Personality and Contribution* (Cambridge Mass., Sci-Art Publishers, 1942), 47. See David Hume, *Treatise of Human Nature*, appendix to Bk. I, 559–60, in Perry, *Thought and Character*, 1: 568–9). It is also notable that T.H. Greene's 299-page introduction to the first volume of James's copy of the *Treatise* – which, Perry points out, makes much of the inadequacy of Hume's philosophy on the matter of relations – seems to have been the object of even closer attention by James than the overall text of the *Treatise* itself. See Perry, *Thought and Character*, 1: 551. Hume's atomism had been the red herring, James thought, which had drawn modern critical philosophy off the scent of sound epistemology. Atomism lies behind the inadequacies of Hume's position on substance (James, *Essays in Radical Empiricism and A Pluralistic Universe* [New York: Longmans, Green, 1942], 42; *Some Problems of Philosophy* [Cambridge, Mass.: Harvard University Press, 1979], 66; Daniel W. Bjork, *William James: The Center of His Vision* [New York: Columbia University Press, 1988], 43–4), self (James, *Collected Essays and Reviews*, 435; *Pragmatism*, 69), and causality (James, *Collected Essays and Reviews*, 435). Hume's positions on these subjects are deeply indebted to his inability to find the origins of relations in something other than the synthetic activities of mind. This a function of Hume's neglect of immediate experience (James, *Essays in Radical Empiricism*, 44). Immediate experience is not fully and accurately represented by abstract reflection upon it, for a crucial shift takes place in the character of immediate experience when it becomes the object of reflection. In its most primitive form, as I will explore more fully below, experience is not constituted by discreet fragments of mental life which must be inferentially or in some other way phenomenalistically 'bundled' together. Rather, relations, as much as relata, are given. Critical philosophy is distracted from this by Hume's philosophical atomism, his recurrent tendency 'to do away with the connections of things, and to insist most on the disjunctions' (ibid., 43) and his contention that '"all our distinct perceptions are distinct existences, and ... the mind never perceives any real connection among distinct existences"' (ibid., 103). Such an approach to experience, while sometimes useful (James, *Principles,*

1: 236), nevertheless 'entirely misrepresents the natural appearances' (ibid., 237). Regarding Kant and critical philosophy in this
respect see Henry James, ed., *The Letters of William James*, 2 vols.
(London: Longmans, Green, 1920), 2: 179; Frederick J. Down Scott,
ed., *William James: Selected Unpublished Correspondence 1885–1910*
(Columbus: Ohio State University Press, 1986) 251.

49  Scott, ed., *Correspondence*, 533. As I indicate below, James's convictions in this respect predated his exposure to Bergson.

50  Seigfried, *Chaos and Context*, 51.

51  Ibid.

52  Myers, *William James: His Life and Thought*, 322–3.

53  Ibid., 322.

54  Ibid., 333.

55  Ibid., 314.

56  James, *Some Problems of Philosophy*, 58.

57  Ibid, 59. See also 31, 34, 56.

58  Seigfried, *Reconstruction*, 139.

59  Ibid., 167.

60  Peter H. Hare, 'Introduction,' xxxviii.

61  Ibid., xxxviii.

62  Myers, *William James: His Life and Thought*, 326.

63  Ibid., 338.

64  Ibid., 335.

65  Ibid., 338.

66  Ibid.

67  Ibid., 337.

68  Ibid., 330. Perry offers the following assessment. James, he says, if
he had lived longer,

would have described a sequence of happenings in which events
occur like strokes or pulses, with a thrust of their own; but in
which they would at the same time be continuous – in the sense
of conjunction of nextness, rather than in the sense of connection.
Their continuity would not consist in the link between them, but
in the *absence* of any such intermediary. Being thus in direct contact, they would be subject to 'osmosis.' Event *a* would look forward to, and in some measure anticipate, *b*; *b*, when it came,
would in some measure fulfil this anticipation, and look back

upon *a*. The prospect of *a*, and the retrospect of *b*, would overlap; *a* would be qualified by *b*-about-to-come, and *b* by *a*-just-past. This would not contradict the discrete order of dynamic beats or initiatives: they would begin apart, and run together. Nor would the progressive character of the change contradict the requirements of freedom. Each event would come as an unfolding, as something 'called-for,' or 'looked-for,' but would also have in it an element of surprise. (Perry, *Thought and Character*, II: 666)

69  Myers, *William James: His Life and Thought*, 337.
70  Ibid., 337.
71  Ibid., 310.
72  James, *Pluralistic Universe*, 291–2.
73  Ibid., 286.
74  Ibid., 282; 284, 287. See also James, *Some Problems of Philosophy*, 49.
75  James, *Some Problems of Philosophy*, 54, 55, 59, 61. See also *Essays in Radical Empiricism*, 145.
76  James, *Essays in Radical Empiricism*, 194
77  Ibid., 26.
78  Ibid., 57; 75.
79  James, *Pluralistic Universe*, 292.
80  Ibid., 351.
81  Ibid., 349.
82  Hare, 'Introduction,' xxxvii.
83  James, *Pluralistic Universe*, 284.
84  Hare, 'Introduction,' xl.
85  Ibid., xxxix.
86  Wild, *Radical Empiricism*, 411.
87  Ibid., 338.
88  Ibid., 342.
89  Seigfried, *Reconstruction*, 293.
90  James, 'Will to Believe,' 99.
91  Ibid., 106.
92  Ibid.
93  Letter of W. James to Mark Baldwin, 1899, in Perry, *Thought and Character*, 2: 243
94  Letter of W. James to R.B. Perry, 4 Aug. 1907, in Perry, *Thought and Character*, 475.

95 Myers, *William James: His Life and Thought*, 315.
96 C.G. Prado, *The Limits of Pragmatism* (New Jersey: Humanities Press International, 1987), 159.
97 Ibid., 160.
98 Edie, *William James and Phenomenology,* 70–1.
99 James, *Principles*, 2: 637.
100 Ibid., 619.
101 Ibid.
102 Ibid., 640.
103 C.D. Broad, *Religion, Philosophy and Psychical Research* (London: Routledge & Kegan Paul, 1930).
104 James, 'Will to Believe,' 108.
105 Ibid., 107.
106 Linda Zagzebski, 'Religious Knowledge and the Virtues of the Mind,' in *Rational Faith: Catholic Responses to Reformed Epistemology* (Notre Dame, Indiana: University of Notre Dame Press, 1993), 199–225.
107 James, '1903 Notebook,' in Perry, *Thought and Character*, 2: 700.
108 James, 'Moral Philosopher,' 81.

**4: The Strenous Mood**

1 James, 'Moral Philosopher,' 84.
2 Ibid., 85.
3 Ibid.
4 Ibid.
5 Ibid.
6 Ibid.
7 Ibid., 86.
8 James, *The Varieties of Religious Experience*, 119–20.
9 William James, *Essays on Faith and Morals*, ed. Ralph Barton Perry (Cleveland: Meridian Books, 1962), 83.
10 James, 'The Moral Philosopher,' 85.
11 James, *The Varieties of Religious Experience*, 219.
12 Ibid., 139.
13 Ibid.
14 Ibid., 210.
15 Ibid.

16  Ibid., 285.
17  Ibid.
18  Ibid., 293.
19  Ibid.
20  Ibid., 292.
21  James, 'Will to Believe,' 108.
22  James's resistance to the domination of ethics by theory, in defer-
    ence to the unity of the many elements in actual moral experience,
    including the strenuous mood, sets his position in a distinctive
    relation to significant strands of contemporary thought. In *Ethics
    and the Limits of Philosophy*, for example, Bernard Williams has
    drawn attention to the extent to which a certain form of reflection
    has been brought to bear upon virtually every aspect of life in the
    West, especially in the centuries since the emergence of the modern
    sciences. Such reflection is dominated by the production of *theory*.
    One of the results of the domination of theory in ethics is the dis-
    placement of living, culturally embodied beliefs about virtue, vice,
    and so on – which are 'thick' with conduct-guiding force – with
    'thin' theoretical accounts of these notions. While such thin concep-
    tions appear to lend themselves readily to the convergence of
    opinion prized by scientific culture, they do not *move* people, even
    if they are true.
       This is an old problem, albeit one which has recently become
    more critical. Plato recognized that 'the political problem of making
    the ethical into a force was the problem of making society embody
    the rational justification (Bernard Williams, *Ethics and the Limits of
    Philosophy* [Cambridge, Mass: Harvard University Press, 1985], 27).
    The same challenge confronts contemporary thought. It stands, for
    example, before Roderick Firth's celebration of impartiality in his
    Ideal Observer theory. 'If the observer is not given some motivation
    in addition to his impartiality, there is no reason why he should
    choose anything at all' (Williams, ibid., 84). It confronts Hans
    Jonas's response to the failure of ethical theory to have sufficient
    impact on contemporary behaviour in domains of social justice and
    environmental responsibility (Hans Jónas, *The Imperative of Respon-
    sibility: In Search of an Ethics for the Technological Age* [Chicago: Uni-
    versity of Chicago Press, 1984]).
       The gap between theory and the embodiment of values directs

philosophical attention and effort to the task of bridge-building. Jonas, for example, recommends an affective one:

> A theory of responsibility, as any ethical theory, must deal both with the rational ground of obligation, that is, the validating principle behind the claim to a binding 'ought,' and with the psychological ground of its moving the will, that is, of an agent's letting it determine his course of action. This is to say that ethics has an objective side and a subjective side, the one having to do with reason, the other with emotion ... Without our being, at least by disposition, responsive to the call of duty in terms of feeling, the most cogent demonstration of its right, even when compelling theoretical assent, would be powerless to make it a motivating force. (Jonas, ibid., 85)

So important is sentiment, for Jonas, that he is prepared to say that 'this sheer fact of feeling ... is ... the cardinal datum of the moral life and, as such, implied in the "ought" itself,' even though it is authorized 'from beyond itself' (ibid., 86). At bottom, then, 'the gap between abstract validation and concrete motivation must be bridged by the arc of sentiment, which alone can sway the will. The phenomenon of morality rests *a priori* on this correlation, even though one of its members is only *a posteriori* given as a fact of our existence: the subjective presence of our moral interest' (ibid., 86). The basic scenario is clear. We are faced with a separation of 'abstract validation and concrete motivation.' Sentiment is somehow to be *added* 'from beyond.' Bridge-building is the order of the day.

James, by contrast, does not embark on bridge-building, because from the outset he resists the subservience of ethical thought to theory, and the compartmentalization of intellect, volition, affect, and agency which makes bridge-building necessary, as I will indicate in the following pages.

23 William James, 'Moral Philosopher,' 141.
24 Ibid., 148.
25 Ibid., 153.
26 Ibid., 155.
27 Ibid., 155–6.
28 Ibid., 157.

29 Iris Murdoch, *The Sovereignty of Good* (London: Ark Paperbacks, 1970), 15.
30 Ibid., 7.
31 Ibid., 23.
32 Ibid., 53.
33 Ibid., 35.
34 Ibid., 49.
35 Ibid., 29.
36 Ibid.
37 Ibid., 25.
38 Ibid., 33.
39 William James, 'On a Certain Blindness in Human Beings,' in McDermott, ed., *Writings of William James*, 642.
40 Ibid., 635.
41 Ibid., 640.
42 Ibid.
43 Ibid., 635.
44 Ibid.
45 Ibid., 637.
46 Murdoch, *Sovereignty,* 73.
47 Ibid., 42.
48 Ibid., 38.
49 Ibid., 38.
50 Ibid., 37.
51 Ibid.
52 Ibid.
53 Ibid.
54 Ibid. 42.
55 William James, *Psychology: Briefer Course* (New York: Collier Books, 1962), 424.
56 Ibid., 444–5.
57 Ibid., 442–3.
58 Ibid., 445.
59 Ibid., 424.
60 William James, 'The Energies of Men,' in McDermott, ed., *Writings of William James*, 680.
61 James, *Briefer Course*, 427.
62 Ibid., 428.

63  Ibid., 447–8.
64  Ibid., 448.
65  Ibid.
66  Ibid., 446–7.
67  Ibid., 444–5.
68  Ibid., 450.
69  James, 'A Certain Blindness,' 637.
70  James, 'Moral Philosopher,' 151.
71  Ibid.
72  Ibid., 154.
73  Ibid., 159.
74  James, 'A Certain Blindness,' 645.
75  James, 'Moral Philosopher,' 150.
76  Ibid., 151.
77  Ibid., 142.
78  Wernham, *Heretical*, 102.
79  Ibid., 20.
80  Ibid., 103.
81  Ibid.
82  James, 'Moral Philosopher,' 85.
83  Ibid., 86.
84  Ibid., 84.
85  Gordon Zahn, *In Solitary Witness: The Life and Death of Franz Jäggerstätter* (London: Chapman, 1966).
86  James, 'Moral Philosopher,' 85.
87  James, 'Will to Believe,' 124.
88  James, *The Varieties of Religious Experience*, 394–5.
89  Ibid., 359.
90  Wernham, *Heretical*, 50.
91  Ibid., 102.
92  Ibid.
93  Ibid., 101.
94  Ibid., 78.
95  James, 'Will to Believe,' 91.
96  Ibid.
97  Wernham, *Heretical*, 76.
98  Ibid.
99  Ibid., 76.

100  Blaise Pascal, *Pascal's Pensées* (London: J.M. Dent and Sons, 1932), 68.

101  Ibid.

102  James, 'Will to Believe,' 91.

103  Wernham, *Heretical*, 95.

104  Ibid., 103.

105  James, 'Moral Philosopher,' 86.

106  Ibid., 85.

107  Ibid., 86.

108  James, *The Varieties of Religious Experience*, 386.

109  Ibid.

110  Ibid., 393.

111  C.D. Broad, *Religion, Philosophy, and Psychical Research* (London: Routledge and Kegan Paul, 1930); Martin Buber, *I and Thou* (New York: Charles Scribner's Sons, 1970); Rudolf Otto, *The Idea of the Holy*; W.T. Stace, ed., *The Teachings of the Mystics* (New York: New American Library of World Literature, 1960); A.E. Taylor, 'The Vindication of Religion,' in *Essays Catholic and Critical*, ed. Edward Gordon Selwyn (New York: MacMillan, 1926), 70–80; R.C. Zaehner, *Mysticism, Sacred and Profane* (London: Oxford University Press, 1961).

112  James, *The Varieties of Religious Experience*, 15.

113  Ibid., 66.

114  Ibid.

115  Ibid., 201.

116  Ibid., 302.

117  Ibid., 163.

118  Ibid., 401.

119  Myers, *William James: His Life and Thought*, 457.

120  Ibid., 461.

121  Ibid.

122  Plato, *Republic*, 401d–403c, *Laws*, 652–60a; Aristotle, *Nichomachean Ethics*, 1095a–b, 1104a–b; Augustine, *City of God*, XV, 22. See James, *Essays in Radical Empiricism*, 143, 150.

123  See Alvin Plantinga, *Warrant and Proper Function* (New York: Oxford University Press, 1993); *Warrant: The Current Debate* (New York: Oxford University Press, 1993); 'Why We Need Proper Function,' *Nous* (March 1993).

124 James, 'Will to Believe,' 108.
125 Ibid., 107.
126 Ibid.
127 Myers, *James: Life and Thought*, 456–7.
128 James, 'Moral Philosopher,' 84.

## Conclusion

1 James, *Pragmatism*, 121.
2 John McDowell, *Mind and World* (Cambridge: Harvard University Press, 1994), 24.
3 Gerald Myers, *William James: His Life and Thought*, 343.
4 James, '1903 Notebook,' in Perry, *Thought and Character*, 2: 700.
5 Nicholas Woltersdorff, 'introduction,' to *Faith and Rationality: Reason and Belief in God*, ed. Alvin Plantinga and Nicholas Woltersdorff (Notre Dame: University of Notre Dame Press, 1983), 76–7.
6 William Alston, *Perceiving God: The Epistemology of Religious Experience* (Ithaca: Cornell University Press, 1991), 149, 155.
7 Henry Dumery, *Le probleme de Dieu* (Paris, 1957), 15. Louis Dupré, *The Other Dimension*, 113.
8 John Hick, *An Interpretation of Religion: Human Responses to the Transcendent* (New Haven: Yale University Press, 1989), 213.
9 Terence Penelhum, *God and Skepticism: A Study in Skepticism and Fideism* (Dordrecht, Boston, Lancaster: D. Reidel Publishing, 1983), chapters 6 and 7.

# Bibliography

**Primary Sources**

*Collected Essays and Reviews*. London: Longmans, Green, 1920.

*Essays in Philosophy*. Cambridge, Mass.: Harvard University Press, 1978.

*Essays in Pragmatism*. Edited by Alburey Castell. New York: Hafner, 1948.

*Essays in Radical Empiricism*. London: Longmans, Green, 1912.

*Essays in Radical Empiricism and A Pluralistic Universe*. Edited by Ralph Barton Perry. New York: Longmans, Green, 1942.

*Essays on Faith and Morals*. Edited by Ralph Barton Perry. Cleveland: Meridian Books, 1962.

*Human Immortality: Two Supposed Objections to the Doctrine*. Boston: Houghton, Mifflin, 1898.

*The Meaning of Truth*. Cambridge, Mass. and London, England: Harvard University Press, 1975.

*Memories and Studies*. Edited by Henry James, Jr. New York: Longmans, Green, 1911.

*The Moral Equivalent of War and Other Essays; and Selections From Some Problems of Philosophy*. Edited by John K. Roth. New York: Harper and Row, 1971.

*The Moral Philosophy of William James*. Edited by John K. Roth. New York: Apollo Editions, 1969.

*A Pluralistic Universe*. Edited by Frederick H. Burkhardt. Cambridge: Harvard University Press, 1977.

*Pragmatism.* Edited by Fredson Bowers and Ignas K. Skrupskelis. Cambridge: Harvard University Press, 1975.

*The Principles of Psychology.* 2 volumes. New York: Henry Holt, 1890.

*Psychology. Briefer Course.* New York: Collier Books, 1962.

*Some Problems of Philosophy.* Cambridge: Harvard University Press, 1979.

*Talks to Teachers on Psychology: and to Students on Some of Life's Ideals.* New York: Henry Holt, 1899.

*The Varieties of Religious Experience.* Cambridge: Harvard University Press, 1985.

*William James: The Essential Writings.* Edited by Bruce W. Wilshire. New York: Harper Torchbooks, 1971.

*The Will to Believe and Other Essays in Popular Philosophy.* Ed. by Frederick H. Burkhardt, Fredson Bowers, Ignas K. Skrupskelis. Intro. by Edward H. Madden. Cambridge: Harvard University Press, 1979.

*The Writings of William James.* Edited with an introduction by John J. McDermott. New York: Random House, 1977.

**Letters of William James**

Hardwick, Elizabeth, ed. *The Selected Letters of William James.* New York: Farrar, Straus and Cudahy, 1961.

James, Henry, ed. *Letters of William James.* London: Longmans, Green, 1920.

Kaufman, Marjorie K. 'William James's Letters to a Young Pragmatist [H.V. Knox].' *Journal of the History of Ideas,* 24 (1963): 413–21.

Kenna, J. C. 'Ten Unpublished Letters from William James, 1842–1910, to Francis Herbert Bradley, 1846–1924.' *Mind,* 75 (July 1966): 309–31.

Le Clair, Robert C., ed. *The Letters of William James and Theodore Flournoy.* Madison: University of Wisconsin Press, 1966.

McDermott, John J., gen. ed. *The Correspondence of William James.* Charlottesville: University Press of Virginia, 1992, 1993, 1994, 1995.

Nethery, Wallace, ed. 'Pragmatist to Publisher: Letters of William James to W.T. Harris.' *Personalist,* 49 (Fall 1968): 489–508.

Perry, Ralph Barton. *The Thought and Character of William James.* 2 volumes. Boston: Little, Brown, 1935.

Scott, Frederick J. Down, ed. *William James: Selected Unpublished Correspondence, 1885–1910.* Columbus: Ohio State University Press, 1986.

## Secondary Sources

Alston, William. *Perceiving God: The Epistemology of Religious Experience.* Ithaca: Cornell University Press, 1991.

Aristotle. *The Basic Works of Aristotle.* Edited by Richard McKeon. New York: Random House, 1941.

Augustine, *The City of God.* 2 volumes. Translated by John Healey Tasker. London: J.M. Dent and Sons, 1945.

Ayer, A.J. *The Origins of Pragmatism. Studies in the Philosophy of Charles Sanders Peirce and William James.* San Francisco: Freeman, Cooper, 1968.

Bain, A. 'Belief.' *Chambers Encyclopedia.* London: W. and R. Chambers, 1861.

– *Mental and Moral Science.* 3rd edition (1872). London: Longmans, Green, 1879.

Barrett, William, and Aiken, Henry, eds. *Philosophy in the Twentieth Century.* New York: Random House, 1962.

Bjork, Daniel W. *William James: The Center of His Vision.* New York: Columbia University Press, 1988.

Broad, C. D. *Religion, Philosophy, and Psychical Research.* London: Routledge and Kegan Paul, 1930.

Buber, Martin. *I and Thou.* Trans. by Walter Kaufmann. New York: Charles Scribner's Sons, 1970.

Chakrabarti, Chandana. 'James and the Identity Theory.' *Behaviorism,* 3 (Fall 1975): 152–5.

Clifford, William Kingdom. *Lectures and Essays.* London: MacMillan, 1886.

Davis, S.T. 'Wishful Thinking and "The Will to Believe."' *Transactions of the Charles S. Peirce Society,* 8 (1972): 231–45.

Dewey, John. 'What Pragmatism Means by Practical.' Reprinted in *Essays in Experimental Logic.* New York: Dover Publications, 1953, 303–34.

Dumery, Henry. *Le Probleme de Dieu.* Paris: Desclée de Brower, 1957.

Dupré, Louis. *The Other Dimension: A Search for the Meaning of Religious Attitudes.* New York: Doubleday, 1972.

Earle, W.J. 'James, William.' *The Encyclopedia of Philosophy.* 8 volumes. New York: Macmillan and The Free Press, 1967: 240–9.

Edie, James M. *William James and Phenomenology.* Bloomington: Indiana University Press, 1987.

Freud, Sigmund. *The Future of an Illusion*. Translated by W.D. Robson-Scott. Garden City, N.Y.: Doubleday, 1961.

Hare, Peter H. Introduction to *Some Problems of Philosophy*, by William James. Cambridge: Harvard University Press, 1979.

Hare, Peter H., and Chakrabarti, Chandana. 'The Development of William James's Epistemological Realism.' In Maurice Wohlgelernter, ed. *History, Religion, and Spiritual Democracy*. New York: Columbia, 1980.

Hare, Peter H., and Madden, Edward H. 'William James, Dickinson Miller and C. Ducasse on the Ethics of Belief.' *Transactions of the Charles S. Peirce Society*, 4 (Fall 1968): 115–29.

Henle, Paul. 'William James: Introduction.' In Max H. Fisch, ed. *Classic American Philosophers* (New York: Appleton-Century-Crofts, 1951), 115–27.

Hick, John. *An Interpretation of Religion: Human Responses to the Transcendent*. New Haven: Yale University Press, 1989.

– 'Modern Voluntarist Views of Faith.' In *Faith and Knowledge*. 2nd edition. London: MacMillan, 1967.

Hume, David. *A Treatise of Human Nature*, ed. L.A. Selby-Bigge. Oxford: Clarendon Press 1888.

Kauber, Peter. 'The Foundations of James's Ethics of Belief.' *Ethics*, 84 (January 1974): 151–66.

Kauber, Peter, and Hare, P.H. 'The Right and Duty to Will to Believe.' *Canadian Journal of Philosophy*, 4 (December 1974): 327–43.

Kaufmann, W. *Critique of Religion and Philosophy*. Garden City: Anchor Books, 1961.

Kennedy, Gail. 'Pragmatism, Pragmaticism and the Will to Believe – A Reconsideration.' *The Journal of Philosophy*, 55 (July 1958): 573–88.

Lovejoy, Arthur O. 'The Thirteen Pragmatisms. I and II.' *The Journal of Philosophy*, 5 (January 1908): 5–12; 29–39.

Madden, Edward H. 'Chauncey Wright and the Concept of the Given.' *Transactions of the Charles S. Peirce Society*, 8 (Winter 1972): 48–52.

– 'Discussing James and Peirce with Meyers.' *Transactions of the Charles S. Peirce Society*, 25 (Spring 1989): 123–49.

– Introduction to *The Will to Believe and Other Essays in Popular Philosophy*, by William James. Cambridge: Harvard University Press, 1979, xi–xxxviii.

Madden, Edward H., and Chakrabarti, Chandana. 'James' "Pure

Experience" versus Ayer's "Weak Phenomenalism."' *Transactions of the Charles S. Peirce Society*, 12 (Winter 1976): 3–17.

Madden, Marion, and Madden, Edward. 'William James and the Problem of Relations.' *Transactions of the Charles S. Peirce Society*, 14 (Fall 1978): 227–47.

Mavrodes, George. 'James and Clifford on "The Will to Believe."' In K. E. Yandell, ed., *God, Man and Religion*. New York: McGraw Hill, 1973, 524–8.

McDermott, John J., ed. *The Writings of William James*. New York: Random House, 1977.

McDowell, John. *Mind and World*. Cambridge: Harvard University Press, 1994.

Meyers, Robert G. 'Ayer on Pragmatism.' *Metaphilosophy*, 6 (January 1975): 44–53.

– 'Meaning and Metaphysics in James.' *Philosophy and Phenomenological Research*, 31 (March 1971): 369–80.

– 'Natural Realism and Illusion in James's Radical Empiricism.' *Transactions of the Charles S. Peirce Society*, 5 (Fall 1969): 211–23.

– 'The Roots of Pragmatism: Madden on James and Peirce.' *Transactions of the Charles S. Peirce Society*, 25 (Spring 1989): 85–123.

Miller, D.S. 'James's Doctrine of "The Right to Believe."' *The Philosophical Review*, 51 (1942): 541–58.

– '"The Will to Believe" and the Duty to Doubt.' *International Journal of Ethics*, 9 (1898–9): 169–95.

Murdoch, Iris. *The Sovereignty of Good*. London: Ark Paperbacks, 1970.

Muyskens, J.L. 'James' Defense of a Believing Attitude in Religion.' *Transactions of the Charles S. Peirce Society*, 10 (1974): 44–53.

Myers, Gerald E. *In The Spirit of William James*. Westport, Conn.: Greenwood Press, 1979.

– *The Thought and Character of William James*. New York: George Braziller, 1954.

– *William James: His Life and Thought*. New Haven: Yale University Press, 1986.

Otto, Rudolf. *The Idea of the Holy*. Translated by John W. Harvey. London: Oxford University Press, 1923.

Pascal, Blaise. *Pascal's Pensées*. London: J.M. Dent, 1932.

Penelhum, Terence. *God and Skepticism: A Study in Skepticism and Fideism*. Dordrecht: D. Reidel, 1983.

Perry, Ralph Barton. *In the Spirit of William James*. Bloomington: Indiana University Press, 1958.
- *Present Philosophical Tendencies*. New York: Greenwood Press, 1968.
- *The Thought and Character of William James*. 2 volumes. Boston: Little, Brown, 1935.
- *The Thought and Character of William James: Briefer Version*. Cambridge: Harvard University Press, 1948.
Plantinga, Alvin. *Warrant and Proper Function*. New York: Oxford University Press, 1993.
- *Warrant: The Current Debate*. New York: Oxford University Press, 1993.
- 'Why We Need Proper Function.' *Nous* (March 1993).
Plato. *The Collected Dialogues of Plato*. Edited by Edith Hamilton and Huntington Cairns. Princeton: Princeton University Press, 1961.
Pojman, Louis. *What Can We Know: An Introduction to the Theory of Knowledge*. Belmont, Calif.: Wadsworth Publishing Company, 1995.
Prado, C.G. *The Limits of Pragmatism*. Atlantic Highland, N.J.: Humanities Press International, 1987.
Putnam, Ruth Anna, ed. *The Cambridge Companion to William James*. Cambridge: Cambridge University Press, 1997.
Roback, A.A. *William James: His Marginalia, Personality and Contribution*. Cambridge, Mass.: Sci-Art Publishers, 1942.
Russell, Bertrand. 'William James' Conception of Truth.' In *Philosophical Essays*. New York: Longmans, Green, 1910.
Schiller, F.C.S. 'William James.' *Quarterly Review*, 236 (1921): 24–41.
Seigfried, Charlene Haddock. *Chaos and Context: A Study in William James*. Athens: Ohio University Press, 1978.
- *William James's Radical Reconstruction of Philosophy*. Albany: State University of New York Press, 1990.
Suckiel, Ellen K. *Heaven's Champion: William James's Philosophy of Religion*. Notre Dame, Ind.: University of Notre Dame Press, 1996.
Taylor, A.E. 'Some Side Lights on Pragmatism.' *McGill University Magazine*, 3 (1904): 44–66.
Taylor, Richard. Introduction to *Theism*, by John Stuart Mill. Indianappolis: Bobs-Merrill, 1957.
Wernham, J.C.S. *James's Will-to-Believe Doctrine: A Heretical View*. Kingston, Ont.: McGill-Queen's University Press, 1987.
White, Morton. 'Pragmatism and the Revolt against Formalism: Revi-

sioning Some Doctrines of William James.' *Transactions of the Charles S. Peirce Society,* 26 (Winter 1990): 1–17.

Wild, John. *The Radical Empiricism of William James.* Garden City, N.Y.: Doubleday, 1969.

Wilshire, Bruce. *William James and Phenomenology: A Study of the Principles of Psychology.* Bloomington: Indiana University Press, 1968.

Woltersdorff, Nicholas. Introduction to *Faith and Rationality: Reason and Belief in God.* Edited by Alvin Plantinga and Nicholas Woltersdorff. Notre Dame, Ind.: University of Notre Dame Press, 1983.

Zaehner, R.C. *Mysticism, Sacred and Profane.* London: Oxford University Press, 1961.

Zahn, Gordon. *In Solitary Witness: The Life and Death of Franz Jäggerstätter.* London: Chapman 1966.

# Index

9 781442 614901